Ian McNamara

AUSTRALIA ALL OVER 2

D1489523

ABC
Books

ACKNOWLEDGMENTS

Once again I have to thank several colleagues, friends, experts for their help in making this second book happen. So, Leona, Dawn, Helen, Andrew— thanks for digging up the material, transcribing the interviews, editing and designing with skill, and making me look good on the cover. And Sally's guidance is evident again.

Published by ABC Books for the
AUSTRALIAN BROADCASTING CORPORATION
GPO Box 9994 Sydney NSW 2001

Copyright © Currawong Music Pty Ltd, 1994

First published October 1994
Reprinted 2007

National Library of Australia
Cataloguing-in-Publication entry
McNamara, Ian
    Australia all over. 2.
    ISBN 978 0 7333 0338 8.
    1. Australia—Social Conditions. 2. Australia—Social life
    and customs. I. Australian Broadcasting Corporation. II.
    Title. III. Title: Australia all over (Radio program).
994

Illustrated and designed by Helen Semmler
Set in 11/16 Goudy
by Midland Typesetters, Maryborough, Victoria
Printed in Hong Kong, China by Quality Printing

5 4 3 2

CONTENTS

For The People

INTRODUCTION

Well, here it is, *Australia All Over* the book, Volume Two. The first book chronicled the years 1987–91 and we talked about trains and shopping trolleys, birds and platypuses, Christmas and gumboots, Aboriginal names, signs of rain and much more. We still, of course, discuss these on the program, but like all good things we continue to grow and expand.

This book has a wide range of topics, too, and many of them reveal the concern that Australians feel about some things that are happening in our country—for example, the national debt, wool, small country towns . . . all sorts of things. In letters and phone calls people wonder why our national debt continues to rise, why we can't get a decent Australian-made labelling system in place; why we continue to import so much. And concerns about country towns include the loss of public services such as trains, shopping centres and banks. The following letter from Tony Jakeman of Yarraman in Queensland is typical:

The point the banks miss is that they are no different to car yards, shops or any other type of business—it is just that they are in the business of selling money instead of goods. Unfortunately, the mainstream banks still persist with the concept that they are doing their clients a service lending them money when it is the other way round—the clients are doing the bank a favour by patronising them.

In these pages you'll find a marvellous cross-section of topics that we cover on the program every week—the weather, trees, stars, wool, animals, letters and poems about Mothers and Mother's Day, the story of Hector Conomos of Greek Cafe fame, the feral fivers saga, interviews with 'Oppy' Opperman, RM Williams, Eleanor from Balgo Hills, Bill Fordyce and the much-loved Gilbert. The difficulty I had compiling the book was what to leave out! For example, the poems. I reckon some of the best poetry around is sent to me. My calico bags (environmentally friendly!) contain hundreds of poems sent in over the years. I can only ever read a small fraction of them on the program. Maybe I'll compile another book when I've some spare time!

The Why I Live Where I Live section is again one of the highlights. Every week I receive many letters telling me why Australians live where they do, and it never ceases to amaze me how much real love is expressed for this country. Even people who are suffering enormously in drought-stricken areas can nonetheless write optimistically and with deep affection.

I mentioned my calico bags. I travel everywhere with them. They contain the letters and poems that I read and re-read. They are my constant companions. I receive so many, it can take up to two years for me to read them on air. For example, this one from Margaret Arnett in Wingham, NSW, arrived in late 1993.

Because you are so down to earth and appear to share our dreams and ideals is probably the reason so many thousands of us send you our poems, stories, ditties. We don't send them in hope of hearing them on radio but just to share them with you.

Thank you, Margaret. I know I still haven't used the cricket poem you sent in—but I *will*.

I've been presenting the program now for just on ten years. It's been a long association, but I still continue to enjoy Sunday mornings even though it means a 3.30 am start. Many ask how I maintain my enthusiasm—the answer's easy: I meet so many new and interesting people every Sunday morning. I travel all over as much of Australia as I can, and since the last book I have met thousands of friends at the various ABC Picnics in the Park. It astounds me how many come to those picnics, often travelling hundreds of kilometres to be there. There are some photographs further on that show huge picnic crowds in all weathers. It's all very humbling and I love being there.

The one recurrent theme you'll find in this book is the sense of humour, the smiling-in-the-face-of-adversity spirit that is an essential and totally unique part of the Aussie makeup. And that same theme is repeated week after week on the program. It keeps me going when the daily round gets tougher, as it does for all of us.

Thank you all for your contributions. Without you there'd be no program. I have regular contributors such as Dorothy Watt from Briagolong, Bill Scott from Warwick, Helen Brumby from Tassy and a host of others, but whether you're a regular listener/contributor or not I thank you all most sincerely.

Finally, let me quote from a speech made by Kevin Keady, Coonamble Shire's President. I was opening their archives, and he made a couple of telling points about the program:

There is a warmth about *Australia All Over* that makes it unique in radio today: with its human interest the people of Australia are shown as they really are, a very diverse group—offbeat bushies, larrikins or little old ladies, truckies, drovers, pub keepers, shearers, all sorts of people. There are no political overtones or hidden agenda. Sunday morning is a cheap trip around Australia for those who will never make it due to age, illness or lack of extra cash.

See you all next Sunday!

ANIMALS AND OTHER CREATURES

Nineteen ninety four was a first for me. I patted a wombat called Suzy at the Belair Picnic in Adelaide. She was so beautiful and soft and cute. She was later released in one of John Walmsley's sanctuaries. Isn't it sad that we have to do this, use fenced-in sanctuaries, mostly to protect our native animals from ferals, cats, dogs, rabbits, foxes and, of course, *us*. We are the biggest threat to our birds and mammals, snakes, insects and spiders. We're destroying their habitats. It's something we all ought to think about. Their future is in our hands.

Bilby

The recent mention of Easter Bunnies and Easter Bilbies made me wonder how many people know why we have this tradition. Actually, like Hot Cross Buns and Easter Eggs, it has pagan origins. In the pre-Christian era in Europe there were a host of pagan festivals held to coincide with the full moon—for obvious reasons, because it allowed the party to continue after sundown! With the spread of Christianity, the festival of Easter was superimposed on these, but vestiges of the old festivals remained.

The bunny was not a rabbit at all, but a hare, an animal sacred to the goddess Eostre. The baby hare, born with its big round brown eyes wide open and resembling the full moon, was chosen as a symbol of the moon and fertility, both of which were associated with the goddess Eostre. Perhaps it is appropriate that the Easter Bunny has pagan origins, because there is little of Christian significance in the modern commercial campaigns centred on Easter Bunnies and Easter Eggs—which are mainly directed at children.

From: Norman C. Killeen, Rutherglen, Victoria

In the middle of Australia in a little outback town
Lived a little Bilby who had a little frown
It was drawing near to Easter in that little outback town
Now all the little Bilbies had a little frown
In that little town, the Mayor said it was fair
That 'all the little Bilbies should deliver eggs everywhere'
Now it was after Easter in that little outback town
And none of those little Bilbies had a little frown.

From: Elaine White, aged 9 years, Yarrawonga, Northern Territory

I'm a teacher in a day care centre called Rainbow Cottage in Dubbo. You may be interested in what I have programmed for the children this Easter and that is to promote the Easter bilby instead of bunny. The idea came from your program last year.

The children's program involves discussing the reason for bilbies' near extinction, habitat and what they eat. Craft activities have also been incorporated, along with changing some songs from bunny to bilby. The program extends to the making and selling of what we call 'bilby badges' with pictures and slogans, such as 'Ask Me What's A Bilby'.

We are lucky here in Dubbo to have the Western Plains Zoo who have a bilby breeding program, so it is appropriate that the children will be making visits to see the bilbies and it will be then that the money raised will be presented.

From: **Lesley Crump, Dubbo, New South Wales**

Have a look at the photos of the snakes further on in the book.

I have lived in the bush all my life and have never seen anything like it before. A big brown snake eating another brown snake not much smaller than itself. This took place right in front of my main gate into the house yard. Unfortunately, I didn't see the first encounter, but from the time I came on the performance till the time it finished took about two hours, so I had time to photograph the whole thing. The early stage of the meal consisted of a lot of pulling and twisting until the smaller snake died and was able to be straightened out. Then the eating was much quicker. The last photo shows about nine inches of tail hanging out of the snake's mouth which he couldn't swallow. It then moved off slowly away from my house yard being directed by squirts from a garden hose.

From: **Ken Spinks, Balranald, New South Wales**

Several years ago, while installing a stock watering reticulation scheme on a warm sunny day in a dry tussocky area I saw a hoop snake, about twenty inches in diameter, bowling along with its tail in its mouth, just like a small bike wheel, whirling along through the tussocks—first time I had ever seen one, and haven't seen any since.

From: **Donald Hardy, Warren, New South Wales**

I was unfortunate enough to be bitten by a tiger snake back in February on the day of the big Hobart bushfires of 1967. I was twenty-two years of age at the time and working as a nursing sister in the intensive care unit of Launceston General Hospital.

I had gone home to Launceston from my shift and we had a grapevine growing along our back fence. My Mum used to place bowls of water under the grapevine for our kittens to get a drink. I was poking a twig in amongst the grapevine and the kittens were pouncing and playing. I decided to reach in and pick one up. Imagine my surprise when a big tiger snake lurched out and bit me on the forearm.

I am only four feet ten inches tall, but I hurdled a four foot hydrangea bush getting inside to Mum. Dear Mum wondered what all the fuss was about and when I told her I'd been bitten by a tiger snake she replied 'Wait till I find my reading glasses'. She then whipped the belt off her dress and made a tourniquet, phoned the ambulance and—three months later I was discharged from intensive care.

To say I was crook would be an understatement. I suffered blood clots in the lungs and severe kidney damage due to the blood clots. I ended up with a tracheotomy and was on a life support system for eight weeks. I did recover, after having one kidney removed, and the remaining one is functioning with help from medication.

The funny part to this story came some twelve months later. I was back at work in intensive care when a snake bite victim was admitted. The man had been bitten on the hand and had shot three of his fingers off. I asked him why he had done this. His reply—'I read in the paper last year about a little nursing sister who bloody near died after being bitten by a snake'. I said 'Do you know who I am?' 'No, love' he said. 'I'm that little nursing sister who nearly died'. He said 'What a waste of a bullet'!

From: Helen McLaughlin, Launceston, Tasmania

Recently you had a segment on a Queensland report about raining fish in which one expert debunked the whole thing, saying that the fish were really on the ground and were revived by heavy rain.

I know this can happen but meteorological records throughout the world include many accounts of raining small fish, and not only small fish but frogs, toads and eels. These have fallen down the neck of observers' coats and have been collected in hats as they fell, as well as being found on the roofs of buildings after the rain.

A severe vortex of the tornado family passing over a river, lake or dam with small fish near the surface of the water is usually the means whereby fish are lifted up from the earth's surface. These are later deposited as heavy rain within a short horizontal distance, usually less than fifty kilometres. Although relatively rare, there have been reports of raining fish from all mainland states of Australia and even the desert near Birdsville. There have also been accounts of small farm dams being emptied as all the water was sucked up by a tornado.

From: Allan Brunt, Former Regional Director, Bureau of Meteorology
South Australia

When I was a child my family lived in the Upper Burnett district in Queensland, and from the onset of summer each year there were either dust storms with strong winds or heavy thunderstorms pulling the roofs off houses and sheds, uprooting trees and filling up the river and dams.

The whirlwinds would pull small creatures off the ground and take them up into the air out of sight, then drop them some distance away, always dead. Chickens, puppies, mice, rats and of course anything loose on the ground were fair play for these whirlwinds.

During the late 1950s to early '60s we lived in Townsville, Queensland. One Sunday afternoon, I took my two small boys to the airport to meet my husband who was returning from Mt Isa after a business trip. We had a late summer storm and the tarmac was flooded. Suddenly, the two boys spotted movement in the water, and ran out to see dozens of small fish flapping around. We grabbed a water bottle from the car and caught about sixteen fish, all about three centimetres long. We took them home, and put them in the fish tank with our six tropical fish, then went out for a drive in the cool of the evening. When we returned all but one rescued fish were flapping around on the lounge room floor. We returned them to the tank but they all died after a few days.

From: Margaret Merefield, Herberton, Queensland

In 1944 I was stationed with a heavy bomber squadron at Fenton airstrip in the Northern Territory. Every afternoon very heavy monsoonal thunderstorms would come over, rain and stop just as suddenly, and we used to take shelter under the aircraft. One day it poured as usual and afterwards we walked out on to the bitumen and found little silver fish about two inches long, all dead. We went further and found more on the big airstrip which was about a mile long and a hundred yards wide.

Now, there is no way in the world that those fish swam there from anywhere in that desolate country with no rivers or streams. They couldn't have come from anywhere but the sky.

From: John Hawkins, Springsure, Queensland

I was interested in your item about raining fishes and your remark about raining cats and dogs. I haven't seen either but I *have* seen it raining frogs. On an Easter holiday in Victoria, driving in the Grampians some forty years ago, we ran into heavy rain near Stawell and small green frogs were pelted against our windscreen. They were thick on the ground when we arrived at Halls Gap. They must have been swept up in a willy-willy because the Grampians are a long way from the coast and, of course, frogs are everywhere.

From: Jean Randall, Orange, New South Wales

When my wife and I visited Ayers Rock in 1974 it was a wet season and the Todd was in full flow. I climbed to the top of the Rock and to my amazement saw tiny fish up to three-quarters-of-an-inch-long swimming around in the rock depressions. I even removed a number of cigarette butts from three or four of the small pools in the hope that the fish would survive a little longer without the tobacco.

For years my wife has urged me to make enquiries and perhaps receive a solution to the mystery. However, judging from 'experts' and all the others during your 'falling fish' saga I just can't see a satisfactory explanation ever emerging.

From: **John Campbell, Toormina, New South Wales**

In 1970–71 I was working around the little whistle stop of Duchess, which is about half a day's run down the track south of The Isa. The locals said that they had had a thirteen year drought, but that was the year that it was broken with a vengeance. After several days of steady rain the desert went from dead brown to bright green. A joke went around the Duchess Pub that the cockies were having to force the fresh grass down the throats of the cattle to show them that it was edible!

Anyway, on the second day I was sitting killing time on the porch of the Pub and wondering when I would be able to get back to work when I saw movement in the graded gutter of the track where water was flowing. I wandered out to have a look and, sure enough, that little stream was full of one-inch and two-inch fresh water perch. I called to the dozen or so others in the Pub and soon we were all standing in the rain, beers in hand, heatedly arguing about where those finny things had come from.

The debate went back into the Pub with us. The opinions were split just about evenly. One school had it that they had lain dormant in the ground for all of those years of drought, while the other, including myself, argued that they had come out of the sky. After a while I happened to look over at the Post Office. Now, that building was about thirty feet square and built off the ground on short stumps. But at that moment the important feature of the design was the roof. It was flat and had been made to hold three inches of pumped water for insulation against the desert sun. Because of the long dry it had been years since it had been filled. I got the attention of the group and we filed back out into the rain to get the ladder behind the Pub. Sure enough, the roof was full of water and, what was even more interesting, there were hundreds of fish as well. Now, how did those fish get into that tar-lined pool which had been baked for years by the sun and was a good twelve feet off the ground unless they had come down with the rain?

The hibernating faction went back into the Pub shaking their heads and, while dripping water on the floor, looked into their beers in silence.

The Publican called The Isa radio and told them about it. A while later we listened to the local news report and from the way they handled the item they obviously thought that we were having a real good party at the Duchess Hotel. But none of us who climbed that ladder to look at the roof of the Post Office have any doubt. IT DID RAIN FISH!!!!

From: Captain Richard Coleman, Cairns, Queensland

I still have vivid memories of an occasion in 1943 when we were on an Army survival course on the coast north of Cairns. We had noticed several water spouts out to sea over a couple of days. When one of these funnels of water dissipated over a peninsula we were camping on, it dumped tons of salt water, fish and pieces of seaweed around our position. The fish looked like small mullet about three inches long, and the seagulls had a feast.

Having witnessed many a 'willy-willy' inland depositing various items of debris on land when they petered out, we then surmised that a water spout picked up surface fish etc. in a similar manner, and what goes up generally comes down.

From: Vic Leslie, Kiama Downs, New South Wales

About twenty years ago I was driving along the road near Boisdale, Gippsland, during rain, when small green frogs about one to one-and-a half inches long started falling on the bonnet of the car. Neither my wife nor I could believe our eyes so we stopped the car and, sure enough, the frogs were jumping along the road for about ten metres. They seemed to be unharmed. There were no water holes in the area and they were definitely falling from the sky. I have never related this experience to anybody other than my family for fear of ridicule, so I was very pleased to have my suspicions confirmed.

From: Ray Roberts, Sale, Victoria

One evening when my son was about four years old he had just got into the bath and from the kitchen my wife and I heard him screaming in anguish. Fearing that he had turned the hot tap on and scalded himself we both raced into the bathroom to find him sitting in the bath holding a stiffened frog in his hand.

'Something's wrong with my pet frog', he cried, 'it's gone all stiff.'

He had only wanted to share his bath with his pet but it took ages to comfort him when we told him that because frogs were cold-blooded creatures the heat of the bathroom had killed it.

Further on frogs: around 1940 as a school kid in Wonthaggi a popular winter pastime among the boys was to go 'bullfrogging' in the paddocks over the railway tracks, where depressions filled with water and became home to a vast number of large green frogs whose calls could be clearly heard half a mile away on still, frosty nights. After school and at weekends we would descend on these ponds, shed our shoes and socks, roll our (short) trousers up to the crutch and wade through the water for hours chasing frogs, putting them into jars and taking them home.

Why did we do it? I can't remember. No doubt it was just something to do—the thrill of the hunt.

I never had them for long at home. They always seemed to have a remarkable ability to escape during the night, no matter how securely they were housed.

In hindsight, I bet they received some help from Mum.

From: Len Treweek, Richmond, Tasmania

I worked on a copper mine at Marble Bar in 1959, '61 and '62 and at the mine we passed through an area of quartz rock about two metres wide at 130 feet below the surface. Inside the milky quartz were frogs about three-quarters of an inch long, grey in colour, in a space about twice their size. Once opened or exposed to oxygen they expired. Samples were sent to Perth Museum but I never heard of the results of the Marble Bar frogs, and the mine is now disused.

From: John Crowe, Greenmount, Western Australia

IAN TALKS WITH JULES HOFFMAN

JULES: Last week you spoke with two gentlemen, one was from Kumbia and the other from Townsville, regarding the phenomenon of fish falling with rain.

In 1960 when I was on a business trip to Blackall, I heard from the locals similar stories. Their theory was that eggs laid in dams or water courses were sucked up by extreme evaporation, willy willys or water spouts and presumably due to atmospheric conditions they hatched whilst in the sky.

In the air?

JULES: Yeah and came back as rain.

Oh, right.

JULES: Now, in 1950 I think it was, some friends and myself were going to South Molle. We detrained at Proserpine and because of an impending thunderstorm caught a taxi from the railway station to the hotel. No sooner had we got in the cab than down it came as it does up there, and we heard these plop plop plops on the roof of the car. The headlights were on and all of us could see quite distinctly these little green frogs about the size of between a five and a ten cent piece just falling out of the sky. And we hadn't touched a drop!

That's your story.

JULES: It's true. The taxi driver said it seemed to be a common occurrence up there.

There wasn't someone chucking frogs at you?

JULES: No way!

A friend of mine recently saw a family of wood ducks crossing Bushland Drive, a road on the northern edge of Taree.

The ducklings were very young and when they reached the concrete gutter the little ones were unable to climb the gutter. Mum or Dad realised their problem and one of them lay down in the gutter and the little ones walked over Mum or Dad to the top of the gutter.

This is interesting in itself, but the question is, in these days of equal opportunity, who lay down in the gutter? In my view it was obviously Dad. He would have been old enough to have heard of Sir Francis Drake and his cool thinking in times of crisis.

From: **John Machin, Wingham, New South Wales**

In *The Age* of Sunday the 18th of April was a four-column-wide article plus a large photograph of white cockatoos captioned: 'BIRDS OF PREY: An Australian icon on the rampage in the Victorian towns of Goughs Bay and Bonnie Doon. Several homes have been "attacked".' It goes on to say that as many as fifty birds have been pecking away at the side of one house, shredding the weatherboards, and it adds that they do this because they are 'bored, not hungry'.

The truth is a very different story—it is because their habitat and breeding grounds have been systematically wiped out by the wood-chipping and similar industries. Cockatoos live to a great age and some have been known to live for eighty years or longer. With their habitat gone, they are capable of foraging further afield than many other birds for their food, and this accounts for the large flocks occasionally seen near the suburban areas.

But the breeding season comes around each year, and with their habitat gone they look around for soft timber like the rotting dead branches or tree stumps which they normally tear open to reveal a hollow nesting place inside. With the trees gone, they apparently find weatherboard houses a tempting alternative.

The wood-chippers will say they can migrate to the areas of forest which have not been cleared. But these are already at saturation point and carry the maximum animal and bird life they can support. With the influx of new residents the battle for survival commences and all begin to starve. For several years their numbers have decreased due to lack of food and breeding space.

The authorities are aware of this and approve it because of the short-term gain of a few dollars. But the wanton destruction of our natural rainforest which has taken three hundred years to grow is a wicked and cruel slow annihilation of every bird and animal within the cleared areas.

There seems no valid reason why wood-chippers should not be forced to replant stripped areas, as they do in America, with quick-growing trees which can be harvested after only twenty years. This would eliminate the need to devastate further vast areas of our natural rainforest as is being done at present.

From: Gordon Savage, Pascoe Vale South, Victoria

On hearing on your program of the large numbers of emus around the Broken Hill area I have been prompted to send you a photo taken on the Broken Hill–Menindee road a few days ago. On close inspection you will notice there are many emus in the shot, and if you hold it close to the mike any Victorians and Queenslanders listening will be able to find the white one in mid-photo. To the right a fox is fascinated by the intruder with the 'Richo'. There are large numbers of these in the area due to the fresh supply of kangaroo carcasses found on the roadside. The reason for this is that the 'roos won't obey the unwritten law that you only cross the road with 5,000 of your mates and never alone. (*The photo is on the color page Aspects of Nature.*)

From: Terry Channing, Menindee, New South Wales

Just twelve months ago I was observing birds in a little local reserve at Ocean Grove when I witnessed a sight that left me rubbing my eyes and pinching myself in case I was dreaming. Firstly, I could see long grass beside the mown track waving from side to side. I was curious; my whole attention was fully on the area wondering what was causing the movement of the grass. Presently out stepped an echidna and proceeded to waddle up the mown path. Then came another, followed still by another and again another. Five in all, in single file close together, waddling along the track, sniffing the air and slapping the leather flap of their back legs, making a clapping noise.

I watched them for about twenty yards. The leader eventually turned off the track and back into full grass. Each of the others followed in close pursuit.

I did not understand what was going on at the time for I had never seen anything like it before. Our friend from Kangaroo Island answered that beautifully by saying the leader was a desirable female!

From **Kay Campbell, Belmont, Victoria**

I am writing to seek help on how to get rid of our neighbour's dog. He comes over to visit us about twice a week and does the rounds of the dairy first (where he cleans up any milk left out for the cats) and then up to the house to find any leftovers. Our two dogs go berserk, and rush out and clean him up. But he is the stupidest mutt in Australia and just lies down and takes it, then hops up and wags his tail, and when they are not looking cleans up the leftovers.

We have tried telling our neighbour, Ken, but he reckons the dog doesn't leave home. If you give him a kick in the rear, he just lies down and then comes back and licks your boot.

One time he was over, my son, Brent, grabbed him and tossed him in the cabin of the milk tanker and told the driver to take the dog for a long, long trip. Unfortunately, the next stop for the tanker was the neighbour's. The dog jumped out, wagged his tail, and said: 'That didn't take long to get home, did it?' We then decided to use a bit of psychology. We have started tying labels to the dog's collar and sending him home. Labels with messages like, 'I am Ken's dog and I like to stay home', or 'I am Ken's dog and I like to go for holidays'.

Yesterday we tied a big label on with, 'I have brought my lunch with me, if I look hungry please feed me' and stapled a small packet of dog cubes to it. We found the label about two hundred metres from the house on the track. The dog had got the label off and then turned round and eaten the dog cubes!

From: **Tony Bailey, Simpson, Victoria**

We live in a street where everyone looks after the neighbours. We water each other's gardens and watch for unwelcome visitors while a family is on holidays. The cats and dogs get fed and the pot plants attended to and that's where the frogs come into the story.

Across the street our neighbours had pot plants that needed to be watered and my wife was doing that when she noticed a big green and yellow frog in one of the drainage trays. On lifting that pot she was amazed to find a further two frogs. As this was the first time she had seen them there she decided to turf them out. Of course, I was given the job of disposing of them when she brought them over to our house, so I turned them loose in a shady damp place where there was a pool.

When our friends came home Kathleen went over to have a yarn and got a shock when Jean told her that the frogs had been there for ages and were friends of the family. Feeling pretty bad about this Kathleen made me try to muster the frogs but there was no sign of them, and that made us feel worse. Of course I got blamed for not putting them where they could be found easily!

About two weeks went by—during which we all worried about those frogs— until one day Jean came over as excited as if she'd won Tatts and said, 'What do you know Kath? My frogs are back!' Now I know this is a bit hard to believe, but I reckon those frogs hung about sulking in the place I chose for them until they heard their folks come home. Maybe it took a while for them to pack their swags and head off across the street back to their proper home, but they were the same frogs all right.

From: Fred G. Ward, Bairnsdale, Victoria

On the subject of mice, we have just been to Edithburgh on the Yorke Peninsula with our caravan for a few days. We went over principally to catch fish from the Port Giles jetty, which is one of the major grain loading jetties here. Anyone can fish from the jetty anytime, except when a ship is being loaded.

Anyway—back to the mice. The first night we discovered there was a mouse plague in full force. We had mice get into the van through a quarter-inch gap around the sink drain pipe, and were they noisy!!! We were up and down all night shifting perishables out of the low cupboards—then they even started on the paper wrapping on the tins of food! Next morning we blocked off the hole, but we still couldn't get any sleep because they ran up the annexe and then across the top of the van. Because we have a Pop Top that has canvas and fly wire, we were afraid that they'd eat their way in that way. So I slept with a long stick next to my bed and tapped the canvas every time I heard them chewing. Needless to say we did not stay a third night.

The mouse plague is so bad, stacks of grain and haystacks are ruined in a very

short time. The area around Edithburgh is a good grain growing area and the comment is that until heavy rains come the plague will just get worse. We had beautiful weather, but it's no good for the farmers. We live just south of Mt Lofty in the Mt Lofty Ranges, and we have a millipede plague—but that I can live with after seeing those mice!!

From: Margaret Stratfold, Cherry Gardens, South Australia

You may be interested in an ongoing problem I have with my kelpie sheepdog, Toby. (We live on a farm.) There are many dogs who like to chase cars, I know, but Toby goes one better. His latest obsession is ripping the mud flap off them! To date he has souvenired five. The latest one he collected intact, self-tapping screws and all! We were able to return it to the owner (our friend) to be re-used. It won't worry Toby. It'll just increase the challenge. Other unfortunate cars have chunks of rubber missing from their flaps, leaving the imprint of his teeth (well almost).

From: Max Goulter, Ariah Park, New South Wales

A group of us are considering investing in a large cat ranch out near Kalgoorlie. It is our intention to start rather small with about one million cats, unwanted strays, which will be obtained from capital cities and suburban areas.

Each cat averages about twelve kittens a year; skins can be sold for about twenty cents for the white ones and forty cents for the black. This will give us twelve million cat skins per year (after allowing for a five per cent escape factor). These will sell for around thirty-two cents, making our revenue about three million dollars a year, averaging $10 000 a day—excluding Sundays and holidays.

We can use old-age-pensioners and unemployed youth for labour and a good person can skin about fifty cats a day at a wage of $3.15 per day. It will only take 663 people to operate the ranch so the nett profit will be over $8200 per day.

Now the cats would be fed on rats exclusively. Rats multiply four times as fast as cats. We would start a rat ranch right adjacent to our cat farm. If we start with a million rats, we will have four rats a day per cat. The rats would be fed on the carcasses of the cats we skin. This will give each rat one quarter of a cat. You can see by this that the business is a clean operation—self-supporting and really automatic throughout. From the rat tails we can get four cents bonus from the government per tail, plus other by-products such as cat gut. We also have a standing order from the CWA for claws and teeth.

Eventually it is our hope to cross the cats with snakes, for they will skin themselves twice a year! This would save the labour costs of skinning as well as giving us two skins for one cat. The cats eat the rats, the rats eat the cats and the shareholders get the profits! Let me know if you are interested. As you can imagine we are rather particular who we want to get into this and want as few investors as possible!

From: Neil Durston, Floreat Park, Western Australia

Recently I was driving from Roxby Downs to Olympic Dam and saw a wedge-tailed eagle eating something. That isn't unusual up here except this time the eagle was eating a cat.

Up here domestic cats have to have a collar, bell and tag. I don't know how long the rule has been in, nor if it is policed. I might just add here that I am a cat lover and cat owner. I suppose there is a possibility my cat could end up eagle food, too.

I actually live at Olympic Dam which is about nine kilometres from Roxby. I often go for walks in the bush (staying on established tracks and roads) and love the sound of wild budgies and finches. The only other place I've seen wild budgies is in the Northern Territory.

There are other large birds up here too—some sort of hawk I think. They are lovely to watch when they are hunting. So often you look up and there they are. They are so close you can see their eyes searching for food. A week or so ago a hawk swooped down only about ten metres from where I was standing to grab something. That was in the caravan park where I live!

In closing I would like to say that it seems that having a cat is almost as anti-social as smoking these days. I might have to give up both!

From: Vivienne Lunt, Roxby Downs, South Australia

My son and I went to the opening of the Bendigo ABC Station last Sunday and although it was cold, wet and miserable, as I looked around at the different people watching and listening, I wondered at the amazing diversity before me.

The fact that all of these people came together from many and different backgrounds, some travelling great distances (we only came thirty-four kilometres) shows to me what I believe is common in all Australians—great pride in themselves, others and achievement, no matter how big or small.

You may think that this is totally ridiculous, but I think I may have the answer to those Taiwanese mouse traps that don't work. Well, we have this chook. I call her Chook because that's what she answers to, and I suppose we really don't have her because our neighbour (Max who is seventy-something) has adopted her and feeds her at his back door. Now I suppose that this arrangement may not seem fair to some but Chook eats next door and lays her eggs in here. We get the eggs and Max gets the company; he says she talks to him and I believe him!

Well, back to the mice/mouse problem. Today Chook was waiting at Max's kitchen door when he came home. When he opened the door Chook rushed in, zeroed in on a mouse, and killed it with a few sharp blows with her beak. She then picked up the mouse, straightened her neck and swallowed it whole! The only evidence was the tail still hanging out of her beak. When Max told me this I fell about laughing, making jokes about how he'd turned my chook into a cat and perhaps he should put out a bowl of milk occasionally!

From: Sue Hill, Maldon, Victoria

Looking at the sky it might rain and then again it might not

IAN TALKS WITH NOEL PARKER

NOEL: I rang you about two things. One, you mentioned Jimmy Sharman's tent. I boxed in his tent at the Crookwell Showground in 1931 when I was about fifteen or sixteen.

You fought one of his boxers?

NOEL: I fought two of them and I knocked both out in the one afternoon, and Jimmy got up on the platform in front of all my Crookwell mates and said, 'Here's the future middleweight champion of Australia'.

And what happened?

NOEL: It never worked out that way! But Jimmy Sharman was a great showman. He just captured everybody's imagination with all the pictures on the canvas where the fighters stood and the drums rattling along. He had an old Chinese feller there to look after the money at the door and I think if a fly got in there he'd be lucky! The other thing that I wanted to mention to you is that I've just come back from a reunion in England of a famous squadron, the Pathfinder Force. Have you heard of them?

Yes, I have.

NOEL: It was absolutely fantastic, and the highlight of that was that we were shot out of the sky over the Ruhr in 1942 by a German bloke, and a historian in Brussels got the number off a piece of my aeroplane and traced it back to my aircraft. He also traced the German fighter pilot who skittled us, and I rang him in Berlin when we were over there. The bloke nearly fell off the telephone!

Could he speak English?

NOEL: Oh, yes, he was a professor at the Berlin University. I said, 'You little bastard, you're the bloke that shot me out of the sky in 1942'. He was so excited.

You're pretty excited, too, Noel, just telling me about it.

NOEL: Oh, well, it was so marvellous. Of course, the excuse was that they were trained only to hit the aeroplane, not the people in it. Have you ever heard such rubbish in all your life? You couldn't knock an aeroplane out without worrying about the people.

Tell us what the Pathfinders did.

NOEL: The squadron was formed in August '42. I was in a New Zealand squadron when I was shot down. Our job was to mark the targets with target indicators. We did this out of both Lancasters and Mosquitoes. Of course, there was special equipment in the aircraft to do this which helped the accuracy of the bombing tremendously. The Germans seem to think that if the Pathfinder force hadn't been formed the war would have gone on a lot longer.

Were you a pilot?

NOEL: Yes, a pilot. I'm writing a book and I'm going to call it My Fight to Fly because my old CO was a mad fanatic of boxing and we used to have tournaments every week. I'd finished with the boxing world then—I was starting to get knocked about a bit—but the Adjutant remembered seeing me fight at Rushcutters Bay Stadium and said, 'If you don't go into this tournament against the army you'll go out as a gunner', so I said, 'I'm in!'.

Did you earn money from boxing? I remember Fred Brophy saying 'A round or two for a pound or two'.

NOEL: No, I only went as far as ten rounds in Sydney but I started to get some tough gents there and that was enough for me. I think it was about two quid to last with the fellers Sharman had, and some rough customers they were. The boxing gloves were gravel-rashed and torn—it was a hazardous business.

How old are you now, Noel?

NOEL: Seventy-six. It's a bugger, this business of getting old! But ever since they booted me out from flying civil airlines because I was too old I've been flying light aircraft round the world. If you don't keep busy you're gone. I'm farming at the moment up at Tooborac. If you're up this way, call in and we'll give you the best steak and cup of tea you've ever had.

And bring some boxing gloves!

NOEL: Yes, I'm still interested in boxing.

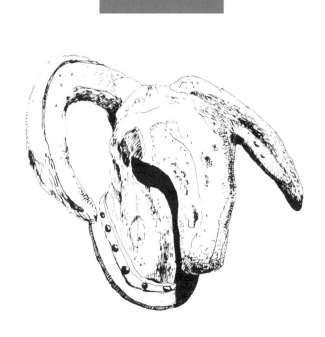

AUSTRALIA ALL OVER

I get a lot of great letters from kids though they come mostly from the country. They love the music, especially 'Bundaberg Rum'—it must be that rude word, 'Gumboots', 'I Took My Trombone to Tamworth' and 'I Made a Hundred in the Backyard at Mum's'. Their letters reflect the hardships faced by country people. This letter from 11-year-old Warwick Benton of Springhurst in Victoria talks about the ever-present drought:

I listen to your show every Sunday. Last week I heard the song about drought. We hadn't had any rain for nearly a month but just as you were singing it started to rain. Unfortunately, it didn't keep going.

   I'd better go now. Keep up the good work.

'I've been everywhere, man....'

SOUTH BANK

It's not far from South Bank to Diddillibah
Grab sunnies, hats, chairs quick hop in the car
We've got to be there as the sun is dawning
On South Bank, with Macca, Sunday Morning

Macca's there smiling, says 'glad that you've come
Sorry you're in for a wet bum'
The flood has gone, but the grass is soaking
On South Bank, with Macca, Sunday Morning

The barbie is on, let's all grab a plate
The smell, oh the smell is ever so great
Fat buns, bangers and bacon are cooking
On South Bank, with Macca Sunday Morning

The crowd grows larger and straw hats abound
Gwen is there, the Lillyput in her hand
Aboriginal names, learn their meaning
On South Bank, with Macca, Sunday Morning

Gilbert is there, we all love you great man
Those tales that he tells as only he can
A big grin and his mind is recalling
On South Bank, with Macca, Sunday Morning

Old people are special, they've gathered the years
The tales that they tell are joy to our ears
Adventure, disaster, all of their living
On South Bank, with Macca, Sunday Morning

We learnt about double doodles, we sang
We smiled and we laughed with all of the gang
With those still at home, we were enjoying
On South Bank, with Macca, Sunday Morning

From: Elaine Holman, Diddillibah, Queensland

I'm writing this in hospital after a hernia op. and the best therapy one could have is the AAO book, which fortunately came out before I went in. Great stuff, Macca, and I was so glad you incorporated a spot on 'Well, I love it!' Jessie.

Since I last wrote to you when I lived in Forrestfield we have moved to Joondalup. I don't know what Joondalup means but it spells a nice place for us. It's about thirty-five kilometres from Perth, a fast growing area but maintaining a fair slice of the bush—blackboys and native trees and shrubs.

My wife, who is of Dutch origin, has just issued an ultimatum to make the AAO book available today for her. Honestly, I almost had to take it into the operating theatre to finish it in time!

From: **Bill and Betty Park, Joondalup, Western Australia**

This is a letter to inform you and your many listeners about the racehorse, Sunday with Macca.

Macca, as he is affectionately called, was purchased as a weanling from the sales at Cornwall Park, Toolern Vale. This sale was held on a Sunday and one of the part owners travelled to the sale from Dimboola and listened to your program on the car radio. He enjoyed the program so much he decided that if a purchase was made the horse would be named Macca.

A weanling was purchased and a list of names all including the word Macca was submitted for acceptance, and the name 'Sunday with Macca' was allotted.

During the colt's stay in Dimboola I was rostered to feed and look after him in the evenings and Peter O'Loughlin was to do the morning chores. The colt settled in quickly and the routine worked well. After a while Macca started to get a little bit frisky, and wasn't unknown to try to shake hands with his back feet. One evening when I was leading him in for a feed he managed to catch me off guard and landed a near back leg on my right shin. I immediately kicked him back and he just stood, amazed, and looked at me. He and I were then good friends and he never had another kick at me.

After he was gelded he was a lot easier to handle, until the time came for him to be floated to his trainer, Bill Sushames at St Arnaud. A float was borrowed from the neighbours and placed ready for an early start the next morning.

Peter and his brother John tried for ages without success to get Macca in the float. The local baker and others were called to help. After some time he was forcibly placed in the float and it was decided to take him up the road to see how he'd travel. After about 300 yards Macca found his way out of the perspex-fronted float and almost onto the boot of the car! A hasty stop in the middle of the road, a lot of frenzied activity, and some time later Macca was untangled from his predicament and put back on all fours. At this point there was loud cheering. To the surprise and embarrassment of our horse transporters a bus had pulled up just nearby and the passengers, who had been watching the activity, were now showing their delight at the rectified situation!

Macca was led back to his yard with a bit of skin off here and there, but not too badly bruised after such an ordeal. It was decided a truck might be the way to shift him and Macca walked into that truck just like an old hand. He was taken to St Arnaud where he was broken in and educated.

Macca had a couple of trials, one race at Murtoa, and is now back in work and should soon race again. We think he may stay a bit, and when we can get him into appropriate races we hope a win will come our way.

Macca's sire is 'Provided (GB)' and his dam is 'It Must Be Love (USA)'.

From: P C Gooding, Dimboola, Victoria

You hinted that you will be doing another *Australia All Over* book. Great, I hope that you go ahead with the project, we all enjoyed your last one so much.

I'd like to bring the following request to your attention: when you do the new book is there any possibility that you give consideration to the actual size and, more importantly, the weight of the finished book? No, I haven't lost my marbles, or not all of them anyway; it's just that Australia Post has strict guidelines on the prices and weights of parcels.

As you would be aware, your last book proved an excellent choice as a gift for both Australian and overseas friends. However, because of its weight, sending it overseas proved a very costly business. I had purchased three copies for friends and relatives in the States and took them to our local post office to catch the Christmas sea mail, but was totally shocked to learn that to post each one would cost more than I paid to purchase it! Naturally, they didn't get posted that day. I took them home and thought about it for days. It annoyed me so much—what do I do now? I've got these three presents that I can't send. With the help of a very sharp Stanley knife I carefully cut the binding and divided the book in two and posted it in two packets. I can't remember the exact cost but it was a fraction of what they wanted for one parcel. When they arrived at the other end they just rejoined them and enjoyed the book!

From: Margaret Craven, Dora Creek, New South Wales

Mate, you won't believe it! This year for Christmas I was given six copies of *Australia All Over*. Six copies! This is a personal best, easily beatin' the three copies of Hugh Lunn's *Over the Top with Jim* I got for Christmas 1991.

What with readin' me six copies, together with the copy I bought at the literary luncheon, I've been pretty busy for the past few weeks.

What to do with me six spare copies is provin' a bigger problem than I anticipated. I can't give 'em to me relatives because they all got a copy for Christmas, too. Me wife, who knows a bit about these things because she often gets a dozen bottles of perfume for Christmas, suggests that I should shove 'em in the wardrobe. She calculates that if they breed like wire coathangers do I should have 124 copies by next Christmas! This will be enough to give all me mates at the pub six copies each. It'll be like a sort of chain book, won't it?

The book is great, Macca, an' recalls many a lazy Sunday mornin' I have spent in your company. Anticipating that you will publish a sequel I have already put in several orders for a new bookcase as a present for next Christmas!

From: **Graeme Murphy, Regentville, New South Wales**

After yesterday morning's beaut show I took down the AAO book from last Christmas and re-read some of my favourite bits—pepperina trees, the Wandering Australorp Swagchook, the Great Maraca Competition, the shopping trolleys and the backyard cricket games. What a lot of fun we've all had over the years, and what a lot of interest there now is in subjects that were once regarded as items for the Lunatic Fringe only. My heavens, I remember driving David Fleay from Burleigh to Brisbane to attend the inaugural meeting that formed the Queensland Wildlife Society back in the sixties. No-one had heard of conservation in those days; now it's taught in schools and a great awareness of our natural heritage is spread across the whole land, thanks in part to your own championship of it through the program, I must add. The point is that sensible people (as most of our fellow countrymen and women are) take sensible views once they know about the problem. *Australia All Over* has tended to inform us of all the concerns, jokes, happenings and interests of our own people right across the country. Your role has been to make the venue available, and the telephone calls that flood in when someone broaches a new topic which is of interest shows that many folk who have encountered the same difficulties and speculations suddenly find they are indeed not alone.

From: **Bill Scott, Warwick, Queensland**

Have just returned from Southbank after sitting there this morning absolutely besotted with seeing you 'live' at last. What a great morning. Those characters that you interviewed just thrilled my soul. Why, oh why can't we be like that today? We live life at one hundred miles an hour and let the lovely things pass us by. Keep up the good work ... you have that rare quality of being a genuine bloke who really loves people.

From: Patricia Sailor, Mount Gravatt, Queensland

Have never written to the ABC, though I've been addicted to your program and others for years. But this morning I had my biggest thrill ever when I heard your interview with Keith (was it Singleton?) at his home in Malvern.

It was his voice. Oh, his voice! The voice of my childhood; the beautiful, natural, fully-rounded voice of my father, brothers, friends and the vocalists of my day. I heard it in the milking shed, around picnic campfires, on Saturday nights around the piano, in singing groups wherever the old songs were loved. And then I heard it in time to marching feet and 'Keep the Home Fires Burning'—the singing sacrifices on their way to Gallipoli, Flanders, North Africa, the Middle East in 1914, 1915 and again from 1939 on. The same voice tones and vowels and volume—the real Australian voice!

From: Roma Cordingley, Bendigo, Victoria

Just a note to let you know how much I have enjoyed your program over the years. I have spent the last nineteen years in Australia and am now returning to England. Needless to say I will miss Australia. Very often I would drive from Adelaide to Melbourne on Sundays and would listen to your show travelling through that vast country, a hundred kilometres without seeing a building—hard to believe as a 'pom'.

I am stopping off in Santorini, Greek Islands, for three weeks and I have been playing a tape of your show. Very naughty to tape your program I know, but I originally took the recording to send it to a friend currently working in a hostel in Beijing who's feeling homesick, and fortunately I had another copy which I brought with me. So, here I am playing your tape on the balcony and the people next door lean out and cry 'Macca'. Yes, they're Aussies. Your fame truly spreads a long way!

The tape is of the program where you told us Mary (with the galah and violin) had died. It still brings a tear to my eyes and I will always think of your program as being the epitome of Australia.

I wonder how the old gentleman who used to exercise on the mat for ten minutes each day is. I think his name was Tom and he used to work on the railways. [Joy is thinking of Gilbert. *Ian*] I can possibly do without barbecues, listening to jazz with a glass of chardonnay, but I don't know if I can cope without 'Macca on Sundays'.

From: Joy Kelly, Brekhamsted, United Kingdom

I am writing to say how much I enjoyed your first book. My family and I were very thrilled that you included Mary's letter re our cricket match on Christmas Day.

The inclusion of the letter was especially significant for us as Mary died on 14 December 1991 from cancer—forty-five years old. However, she left her mark on society as the two schools at Griffith New South Wales where she was a community language teacher both dedicated a school garden of trees to her memory.

She was a great conservationist and loved planting trees. Also, her friends from Sydney dedicated an area and planted one hundred seedling trees at Cecil Hoskins Nature Reserve situated on the banks of the Wingecarribee River near Moss Vale.

This is Mary's letter as we published it in the first Australia All Over *book.*

This morning we heard 'I Made a Hundred in the Back Yard at Mum's' and then at the end of the program you advised us to play cricket today rather than drive on the roads.

We are writing to tell you that our family has been playing cricket on Christmas Day now for thirteen years. True to the song, we play at Mum's, in the side yard rather than the back yard, with the outfielders stationing themselves on the other side of the electric fence in an adjoining paddock.

We use a twelve-gallon drum at the batter's end and a four-gallon drum at the bowler's end. We always bowl from the same end. We don't follow the rule book too closely; in fact most of us don't know the rules, and allowance is always made for either advanced age or extreme youth so that everyone can participate. Three generations take part in the game.

When I was overseas on Christmas Day some years ago the rest of the family lazily sat around saying: 'If Mary was here we'd be playing cricket. I suppose we'd better get out and play.'

We all have a lot of fun; in fact, mirth and hilarity are the order of the day

BYRON BAY

The memorable outside broadcast (OB) from Byron Bay. The big crowd started appearing before the sun came up and by the end of the program several hundred surrounded the broadcast van underneath the magnificent lighthouse. Local historian, Eric Wright, told us all about the lighthouse, and from the top we saw some whales.

THE ULTIMO CONCERT

In December 1993 we held a great concert at the ABC's Ultimo headquarters in Sydney.

. . . .

You can't see her legs, but the lady from the audience is wearing gumboots for the gumboot song (the ones on the table); 'Digger' Revell encourages the folk to join in while the band plays on; and I'm accompanied by a dingo.

and it is very much a Tanner family tradition for Christmas Day. Should you wish to visit us on this day you'd be welcome to join in.

Mary Tanner

It was my birthday on Friday. On opening a gift some good friends had sent me on the last ship (in February) I was pleasantly surprised to discover it was a copy of your book *Australia All Over*. It was also something of a coincidence as not too many days earlier a few of us here at Davis had been discussing your program and how we were avid listeners at home.

The trouble down here, with the time difference, is that *Australia All Over* is all over by the time most of us emerge from our dongas of a Sunday morning. Anyway, it's ANZAC Day today, so I thought I'd drop you a line, or 'wizza' as we call them.

We held a Dawn Service this morning to remember our fallen and perhaps the futility of war. The turnout was excellent with most of the twenty-five wintering expeditioners attending including our three English guests (biologists here for the winter). It was a gloomy overcast morning but relatively warm at minus 15 degrees.

The ceremony was simple with a few improvisations. The gun salute was fired (or misfired) on an old Lee-Enfield 303 carbine and the Last Post and Chorus was played on a mouth organ. The formal part of the day out of the way, we warmed ourselves indoors with the traditional Bundy followed by a sumptuous breakfast and of course a boisterous game of two-up.

I suppose that, as Davis Station is the furthest south of the Australian bases, this would have been the most southern ANZAC commemoration held on the globe.

Cheers from the cold south.

We're awake
for AAO...

I have been over this side of the world for nearly seven weeks and have decided to drop you a line after reading the *Australia All Over* book. I had many laughs while reading the book, which reminded me what a wonderful country Australia is. I have visited England, Scotland, Ireland and France and hope to go to Italy soon. All, so far, have been fabulous places to visit but I have to say my heart belongs in Australia. Travelling over here has made me realise how much there is to see and do in Australia and how much I've yet to see. I will endeavour to see Australia after my return.

Everyone at home listens to *Australia All Over* on Sunday mornings. I come from Barooga on the Murray in New South Wales. It's a small town, but I love it. Since I work in Melbourne I'm always very glad to be going home to breathe some country air—especially that of gum trees and bushland.

Can't wait to tune in on the first Sunday after my return.

From: Nicole Wilton, Sevenoaks, Kent, United Kingdom

Gidday Macca, from the land of the frozen south, where the temperature today is a pleasant minus sixteen degrees at 11.00 am.

I hope by now you have received your invitation to our Mid Winter's Dinner, and hope to phone in on June 20th to discuss the dinner with you on air: in particular, to attempt to give people a little taste of Antarctica at that time of the year. There are nineteen expeditioners wintering here at Casey and we receive Radio Australia loud and clear.

I arrived in Antarctica to take up my post as Station Leader here at Casey in November '92 and will return to Australia in December this year. Over summer our numbers were up to seventy-three people, with a large number of scientific and building programs going on, but since the last ship in February we have been a winter group of nineteen and will remain so until the first ship of the summer arrives in early November. I regard it as a unique privilege to be able to spend a year in this remarkable environment: so clean and unpolluted. The sea is a deep inky blue and from the air you can see several metres into its depths. The wildlife is so tame with little or no real fear of people, which makes for outstanding photographic opportunities. It is also an outstanding place for scientific research and we have winter programs in biology, upper atmosphere physics and medicine. We also have three meteorologists as Casey is Australia's Antarctic Weather Centre. Most of the other people here are involved with either maintenance or communications. We also have a doctor and a chef.

I look forward to talking to you about Mid Winter . . . I like to tell Australians about Antarctica whenever I can.

From: Graeme Armstrong, Station Leader, Casey Station, Antarctica

Recently I took my wife to Atherton for the weekend. After a very nice meal on Saturday night I told her that we needed to get to bed early so we would be up early for Macca. (I don't trust myself to wake up early every Sunday morning so on most Sundays I get an early morning reminder call.) She insisted that it was her right to enjoy the luxury of a sleep-in when she was away for the weekend. She told me, quite bluntly I must say, that if I wanted to listen to the radio at 5.30 am, then I would have to take the wireless outside the room and listen to it there.

I did wake up in the morning at twenty to six and after stumbling round in the dark and messing around with a couple of leads, I did get the radio going and put it on the table outside the Motel room. I sat there huddled up in a tracksuit because it was the sort of morning where a monkey would sing soprano.

It was good to watch the sun come up as I listened to the show and hear plenty of birds responding to the recorded ones coming from the radio.

Just after six o'clock a young Japanese couple strolled past the room as they set off for an early morning walk. They veered away from me and had a little sideways look as they went past. I took my hand out of my pocket, gave them a wave and said 'I'm just listening to Macca, mate'. They both smiled and bowed very politely and kept going at a slightly faster pace. After going for about thirty yards they both turned and gave me a lovely smile and wave before crossing the road.

From: Colin White, Innisfail, Queensland

On the fourth of July we were fortunate enough to have our travels north coincide with your broadcast from Cape Byron. We enjoyed listening to the broadcast and seeing you 'in the flesh'. Very rewarding. But the part we enjoyed most was the people. I found myself having conversations with people I'd never seen before, and I met some who left a lasting impression. One gentleman we met invited us to drop in for a cuppa when we got further up the coast, and he gave us his phone number, which he wrote on the back of a cash register docket. Unfortunately, when we got to his home town of Pottsville, I couldn't find the docket, and since I didn't have his last name, I couldn't even look it up in the phone book. (Sorry, Arthur!)

From: Meg Kerr, Deniliquin, New South Wales

Your book is like Anderson's Fairy Tales
But he knew nothing about cats and snails
You start with birds and you end with trees
And there's a whole bit about Spanish fleas
There's a mixture of rabbits and shopping trolleys
Even frogs and ants get up to romantic follies
And what about those old engines and trains?
And silly gumboots and tropical rains?

There's even cricket and all sorts of games—
I get plain crazy remembering the names
The drawings too are quite remarkable gems;
But the ostriches look like great big hens!
I reckon the book will be a popular hit
Nobody can say they've never heard of it
I'm buying a dozen copies of the blinkin' thing
To sell at the Birdsville Races—and have a fling!

From: **Rex. Fred McKay, Richmond, New South Wales**

AUSTRALIA ALL OVER

(with apologies to Banjo Paterson)

I woke up on Sunday morning, still half asleep and yawning,
Reached out and turned the radio on and fiddled with the dial.
When Macca's voice came booming, I stopped the fine tuning,
And was instantly attracted to his friendly, laid-back style.

As I listen every Sunday, with this land I feel as one, may
I take this opportunity to share my thoughts with you
As each person tells his tale, it never seems to fail,
I get this feeling of strong mateship with your listeners and you.

Oh, your widely-ranging topics, from the snowfields to the tropics
Describe a fascinating country with its wonders and its pains.
Hooray for Gilbert from the railways, and our Aboriginal place-names,
Letters, music, phone and bird-calls, corrugated roads and flooded plains.

A celebration of our culture is *Australia All Over*,
It creates a bond of mateship, as a friend extends his hand,
Macca, you're the one who binds us, so that every Sunday finds us
Glued to 3LO, a radio show, unique throughout our land.

From: **Leonie Weiss, Caulfield North, Victoria**

THE BEST MEDICINE

Hooked up to tubes in hospital
In a strange part of the city,
Away from home and family
And wallowing in self-pity.
The night sky pales behind brick walls
Another day is dawning,
But then a thought comes to my mind
Of course! It's Sunday morning!
I press the bell—'Please hurry, nurse,
It's not a pain attack,
Just turn that switch on for me, please,
It's time for Ian Mac!'

The magpies' song floats round the room,
The callers say 'G'day',
And soon their yarns are taking me
To places far away.
Then Rob comes on with her list of
Events in towns and cities,
Next 'Where I Live', and poetry,
School choirs and outback ditties.

The lass comes in with morning tea
Just as the programme ends.
I've cheered up now, I've visited
My million Aussie friends!

From: **Pat Binskin, Menangle Park, New South Wales**

33

IAN TALKS WITH JIM AND PAT BARRETT

Jim Barrett wrote about the demise of red cedar in Australia and the pocket of cedar he found in the Blue Mountains. He has been a bushwalker since 1948 and he and his wife Pat have walked all over Australia. You see a lot of things when you're bushwalking, Pat. When did you first notice red cedar up in the Blue Mountains?

JIM: It was on my very first trip in 1948. We walked from Kanangra Walls to Katoomba, one of the classic, beautiful walks, and we went through the cedar country and round the Cameron River where the cedar is growing. Later I became interested in how the cedar was taken out of such difficult country and I found that in the last century it could only be brought to civilisation when the rivers were in flood and the cedar logs were made into rafts and floated down to places like Penrith. But the whole scheme came unstuck when one super flood washed all of the logs down to the lower end of the Hawkesbury and the only beneficiaries were the farmers around Richmond, Windsor and Wilberforce who found they had this valuable timber in their backyards.

So the timber-getters cut the wood down and waited for a flood to come.

JIM: They waited for the river to get a little higher than usual, because both the Cameron and the Cox rivers are a series of intermittent pools, or reaches. Of course, when it starts to rain it's very hard to determine exactly how high the water's going to be and the floods in these rivers are horrendous.

You reckon we've got one of the best rivers in the world here. Tell me a little bit about that.

JIM: I've heard people in authority say that the Cameron River is the most beautiful in the world. I would agree with that. It's less than one hundred kilometres from Sydney, it's completely unpolluted, it has become isolated because of the construction of the Warragamba Dam in the 1950s, and substantially it's only available to people who are prepared to go there on foot.

Do you do a lot of thinking when you're bushwalking or do you talk about the scenery?

PAT: We talk about lots of things, other walks you've done ... you think you'll never go on another walk, it's too hard, the pack's too heavy, and then you get to the top of the mountain and you see this fantastic view, and around the campfire that night, 'Wasn't it great!'.

JIM: You just take everything in. You're part of nature. I like to think we've inherited a little bit of the Aborigine syndrome.

Where else have you walked besides in the Blue Mountains?

PAT: We've been to the Northern Territory and up in Kakadu. We mostly go down to the Snowy Mountain region; we've been there in the summertime with the beautiful flowers and, the dreadful flies, and then go back in the wintertime— I'm learning to cross-country ski.

Are you really? That seems to me harder than playing the trombone!

PAT: I'm not really a good skier but I have great fun there, and to get off the tracks and see the fresh snow on the beautiful gum trees—oh, it's just magic!

JIM: In the summer Tasmania and New Zealand are the popular destinations for the more ambitious walker because they represent beautiful country at a time when we normally don't walk. Tasmania would be the walkers' mecca, particularly the south-west; it's just magnificent country. It's a pity in a way that these days most walkers tend to be middle-aged, whereas when Pat and I joined the Club in the late 1940s they were in the eighteen to twenty age group. I think nowadays there are too many distractions, too many artificialities, to encourage people to go out and enjoy what is such a basic pleasure.

IAN TALKS WITH R M WILLIAMS

R M: It's Reg Williams here, Ian.

R M Williams—how are you, mate?

R M: Pretty good. I heard you say you came across the Gunbarrel and there's wildflowers there. Well, in 1926 I came across as camel boy with old Billy Wade who formed Warburton Mission, and there were wildflowers everywhere.

Well, they've had unseasonable rain here in Coolgardie for the last two years—about twenty inches per year. Somebody said the average rainfall's about six to eight inches, so you can imagine what the desert looks like. I don't know what it's like where you are, R M—you're in Queensland, aren't you—it's freezing cold here. But tell us more about your journey. How old were you?

R M: I was only about seventeen. But we had wildflowers up to our knees—I've never seen anything like it.

I'll bet you remember that fondly. Tell me a little bit about Billy Wade.

R M: Old Billy was given the job of exploring that country to find any Aboriginals that needed religion and he made a recommendation that they have a reserve there. It's very big now. It runs from Warburton nearly across to Oodnadatta, almost a million square miles altogether.

How did you get the job of camel boy?

R M: I was building a big old lime and concrete tank for the man who was running Mt Margaret at the time and I got the job then to drive Billy Wade's camels.

You rang us a couple of months ago about Longreach and the old whipmakers you're interested in preserving.

R M: We ran a plaiting school at Longreach and it was a grand success. We're going to have another one of these schools; people like to plait whips.

It was good to talk to you this morning, RM; thanks for ringing.

AUSTRALIAN-MADE AND WOOL

A subject close to everyone's heart. It seems that Australians would love to see their fellows fully employed in Australian industries, buying Australian-made products manufactured by Australian-owned companies. Unfortunately, it's not happening.

This letter from Rhonda and Ian Parker of Tamworth, New South Wales, is typical of some listeners' feelings.

A couple of weeks ago you were saying that if each Australian spent just $50 a week on Australian-made goods our balance of payments would be solved. We used to worry about our trade imbalance and the fact that a lot of Australians are unable to find employment. Since the last election, however, we have concluded that the majority of Australians could not care less about these problems. The government pursues its policy of a level playing field for a game in which other players are prepared to cheat, and at the same time we have a Reserve Bank which will not let our Aussie dollar find its true level.

The combination of these factors and Australia's entrenched, inefficient work practices means that we will never compete with imported goods. We've also concluded that in Australia today work is optional, and that a large number of people have no intention of contributing anything to the economy because the government is quite prepared to look after them in the manner to which they have become accustomed.

So, instead of trying to do whatever we can to help improve our balance of payments, we are now concentrating on the more important issues such as who will be our first President and what colour the flag should be!

I am all fired up to be patriotic and Buy Australian, so I go up to the pub to preach the gospel to me old mate, Fair Dinkum. Well, he is singularly unimpressed and tells me that the Buy Australian campaign has been goin' about one hundred years. When I give a sarcastic, sceptical laugh he takes a long slow deliberate two pint sip of his bucket of beer, hitches up his strides a foot or so an' says 'Listen son'. This always makes me mad because I know I am older than Fair Dinkum, although, if you believe everythin' he tells you he has done, for the length o' time he has done it, I figure he is pushin' 138 years of age and still only a colt! Anyway, Fair Dinkum says 'listen son, old W T Goodge, who died in 1909, wrote a poem called *The Australian* an', fair dinkum, I reckon he musta wrote it about the turn of the century, which makes it about ninety years old, fair dinkum'.

THE AUSTRALIAN
W T Goodge

His clothes are west of England tweed; his boots are from the Strand
The bike which he propels with speed was made in Yankeeland
He drinks a glass of Belgian gin, Jamaica rum, perchance,
And smokes the 'best Virginia' in a pipe that's 'made in France'
He looks at his imported watch to see the time of day,
And hurries, for he wants to see a new imported play.
The lamp is made in Germany that lights him on his way;
He's a patriotic thoroughbred Australian.

He's a patriotic thoroughbred Australian!
And he sticks up for his country like a man!
For it's good for growing mutton but it couldn't make a button
For the trousers of a true Australi-an!

He comes up to his cottage where there's lager from the Rhine,
He seats himself upon a chair of Austrian design.
His English hat he places on a Chinese chiffonier
And he drinks from his Italian glass his German lager beer
He strikes Italian matches and he lights a German lamp
He sees the jam and pickles with the real imported stamp;
He tries the Dutch piano for the latest foreign vamp;
He's a patriotic thoroughbred Australian.

He's a patriotic thoroughbred Australian!
And he sticks up for his country like a man;
And he buys of all creation, bar the land of his location,
He's thoroughgoin' true Australi-an!

Not only need we BUY Australian, but GIVE Australian! Why not have Australian Made goods on hand to be used as Overseas Aid? If the government policy was *Australian Made Only Aid* anything from Southern Cross windmills and pumps to citrus juice poppers could be sent. If there was a government guarantee for the purchase of these and other goods, banks would be able to lend to the production companies, thus putting factories back into production and creating employment.

Australian woollen blankets
Steel buildings
Dried fruit and vegetables
Dried milk products
Dried meat (beef, mutton or buffalo whatever)
Australian cotton canvas tents

These are just a few.

There is also the Australian National Line to ship *our* goods to those less able to provide for themselves or suffering natural disasters. So often this type of aid is needed urgently after a disaster. Government policy should have these goods stored and on hand to be used immediately. The cry should be BUY AUSTRALIAN, GIVE AUSTRALIAN!

I have just returned from a month's holiday in the Northern Territory and South Australia and enjoyed *almost* all of it.

The only drawback really crystallised when I had gone down to Ayers Rock Resort. It is certainly well worth seeing and I was feeling justly proud of the resort, the service and attention to detail and the comfort of my motel. However, I had travelled by bus, and over the period of time I was there I had come to know quite a few of the young Japanese backpackers who were on that same bus. They were very polite and well-behaved young folk and I came upon one of them smiling broadly, with a silk scarf in his hand in the souvenir shop.

When I asked what was amusing him he replied 'Well, you will not like it; I don't think I will tell you'. When I insisted, he showed me the scarf, with a small Aboriginal emblem and the word 'Darwin' printed on it. He said, 'I think to buy it for my mother but I think I won't buy it now'. I asked what changed his mind and he replied, 'Japan Aborigine made it' and showed the tiny 'Made in Japan' sticker. I said, 'Well, perhaps when I go to Japan I'll see that "Australian Japanese" made the souvenirs there'. 'No', he replied, 'they will now allow it. Just Australia. It is great shame for you.'

An American woman beside him listened with great interest and then remarked that she was OK because she had teatowels with Aboriginal designs on them. The boy said, 'Made in Poland. I looked'. Then everyone round us looked at their goods and nothing they'd selected was made here.

What can we do about this? I feel so disappointed, for there is a wonderful adventure awaiting all comers in our beautiful country. They are surely entitled to genuine souvenirs.

From: Heather Hastings, Albion Park, New South Wales

MADE IN AUSTRALIA????

I'm getting suspicious . . . it's nasty, I know
But my confidence dwindles with each low-down blow:
MADE IN AUSTRALIA's displayed on the tin,
But is that the truth about what is within?
Was it only the tin that was made in our land
And was it produced by a true Aussie hand?
And what of the contents . . . from whence did they come?
You just wouldn't know what goes into your tum!
I take my specs shopping, examine with care
Each packet and can and each garment to wear . . .
Then I'm stunned by a thought . . . is it fact or just fable
And MADE IN AUSTRALIA refers *just to the label*????

From: Dorothy Watt, Briagolong, Victoria

My husband and I are 'buy Made in Australia' fanatics but, when we bought food for our cat which was marketed by the RSPCA, we thought we were helping this charity and didn't read the label!!

When I eventually did, I saw RED and wrote and told them exactly what I thought of their support of an overseas company and why couldn't they support Oz industry?

I thought you might be interested in the attached reply. To make things difficult, Macca, what do you do when the cat absolutely refuses to eat canned food that's 'Made in Australia'?

Here is the RSPCA's reply to Mrs Hepburn's letter

The RSPCA and the Vita Pet Food Company have bent over backwards to have its range of pet food all Australian made. Unfortunately, canned fish foods of adequate quality are not made in Australia and Thailand provides human and pet canned fish products for a large part of the world including Europe, Asia and Australia.

This is not a desirable situation and one which the RSPCA hopes it can help to overcome. I have been to the cannery in Bangkok and can tell you that most of the canned fish pet food in Australia is made in Thailand. Ours is exclusively made from sardines caught in the Gulf of Thailand. Driftnets are not used.

As we expand our range of products we will ensure that they are made in Australia but just now it is not possible for the fish product to be made here.

I hope you will relent and continue your support for the RSPCA.

From: Patricia Hepburn, Mount Martha, Victoria

I have listened with interest and dismay to the reports of Australian produce being dumped and wasted because of 'cheap'!!! foreign imports, of businesses going to the wall because they cannot compete with imported goods.

I suspect that the large retailers have a lot to answer for for this state of affairs. They obviously have considerable buying power, particularly when they are members of conglomerate international buying groups. Perhaps we should consider turning this international influence to Australia's advantage.

My suggestion is that any business wishing to import goods into Australia, and where such goods would compete with Australian made or grown goods, then that business must secure their finance for purchasing those foreign goods by exporting Australian products of equal value, or by buying such credit from other exporters.

Next time you visit one of the many Sunday markets that have sprung up around the country, just check out the amount of new imported lines that are for sale. Stall holders buy most of their supplies from so-called manufacturer's agents whose sole business is importing low-priced consumables from Third World countries, much of which is of very poor quality, and pirated copies of successful products produced in countries like Australia, Germany, USA etc.

Whilst we should endeavour to help Third World countries to stand on their own feet, we should make it clear to them that there are certain standards and rules to be observed, and, if they are not prepared to observe them, then we do not wish to trade with them.

In the case of Australian companies who have taken their manufacturing operations off-shore and now import their own products back into Australia, they should be required to pay the same business taxes on their overseas operations as they would if they were manufacturing in Australia, otherwise they would not be granted an importer's licence.

It is time Australia's leaders put Australia's needs first; then the so-called level playing field would slope a little more to our advantage. Presently I suspect it is angled at about forty-five degrees in favour of the rest of the world.

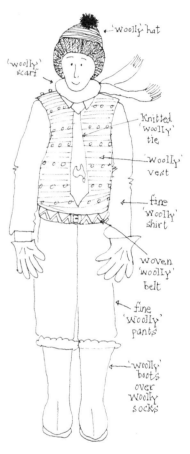

A 'Woolly' Australian

From: Tony Moseley, Dysart, Tasmania

You mentioned that you have your own project to reduce the number of times you have to put out a garbage can. This is good——but you can help Australia in a much more significant way. It is in Australia's short term, as well as long term, financial interest to get every Australian to be aware of what is 'wholly' Australian and what is either just made in Australia by foreign companies or, worse, is fully imported.

Can I suggest to you that you personally have as your project the aim to make your personal purchasing *up to 80% 'wholly' Australian*. Most Australians go out of the supermarket with only 30% 'wholly' Australian items—the rest are foreign.

If you could weave into your program your progress with this project, then you will have a greater impact than all the AUSBUY GUIDES we have issued!

From: Harry Wallace, President Australian Owned Companies Association Limited, Rydalmere, New South Wales

IAN TALKS WITH HARRY WALLACE

Harry, it seems to me that a lot of Australians are concerned about level playing fields and buying Australian. I suppose there are two issues here: one is buying things that are made by wholly owned companies and the other is buying things that are made in Australia. You'd be the first to admit that it's important that we buy things that are made in Australia, even if they're made by an overseas company, but when we import stuff direct from overseas, which we seem to do more and more these days, it really can't be countenanced.

HARRY: If there's an Australian equivalent to the imported stuff available—and, of course, in some cases we don't make the product here—we should never buy the imported thing if we can possibly find it here. Obviously, if it's made in Australia the choice should be that it's from an Australian-owned company. Australia for years has been spending more than it's earned. For the first nine months of this year we've spent about twelve billion dollars more than we've earned as a nation and this year's loss is, in fact, a third worse than last year. We're really having a terrible performance, and out of that loss of about twelve billion, eleven billion went in interest and dividends paid overseas on foreign investment. Our situation is so bad that we really have to save every dollar we can. We have to think of ourselves as a family, not always maximising our own situation, and that's why it's important to buy from Australian-owned companies as well as always ensuring that the product's made in Australia.

There's a lot of things to talk about in this. I've had a letter from Maud Lynd of Joondanna in Western Australia who says: 'This 'Buy Australian' promotion which is so popular at the moment bothers me a little. The way I see it is that if we want to sell our produce—wool, wheat, minerals, etc, overseas—there has to be a reciprocal purchase from those countries. Isn't that balance of payment? If nobody buys these imported goods then our exports are in trouble. Another angle, as I see it, is that we love being charitable to the poor Third World countries and patronisingly give them handouts—why not buy their goods and allow them the dignity of helping themselves, as in footballs from India? Buy Australian by all means if you can afford it, but not to the total exclusion of those who desperately need our encouragement'. What do you say to Maud?

HARRY: Well, that's great if you've got the money. Our banks are in financial trouble now and I'm sure they'd love us to say, 'Look, you're in trouble, we'll pay you a bit more interest', or, when we know that a company's in trouble, to rush and buy their product if we don't need it. The problem is that for twenty years now Australia has been spending more than it's earned, and the critical thing about this is that we've been making up for this by selling off the country, and that's a disaster.

Exactly! I'll read you the last bit of an article by Ken Davidson in *The Age*. You have to realise that this was written before the 1993 election so it talks about

GETTING TO AIR

Getting AAO to air's a real team effort wherever we broadcast. Lisle Smith's the man who gets us to 'air'. 'Where did you say you're calling from?' In their open air 'office' in Launceston, Leona Kelly and John 'Perce' Bamford take early calls for the program; Leona, Roly Mellor, Peter Scott and John smile on a chilly Coolgardie morning — the time is just past eight but we've been up since two-thirty!

KIDS ALL OVER

Wherever we go, kids are great. Aaron and Gerard Maloney, who both suffer from cystic fibrosis, warmed everyone's hearts; when I asked Craig Renneburg, the Principal at Quambone School, 'Is this the choir, Craig?' he replied, 'No, this is the school!' The Launceston Prep choir gave the large crowd top music and smiles; 3R, Gillen Primary, Alice Springs, proudly presented the rainbow rug they knitted for Children's Book Week.

Fight Back and stuff, but you'll get the drift. I think it's very germane:

'The Hawke/Keating government points the way. Qantas AA—Australian Airlines—is now controlled by British Airways. In return for a licence costing some $800 million the Hawke government gave Optus subsidised access to the Telecom network' (that's a 49% American company) 'This has wiped three billion off the value of Telecom and the competitors are already disputing the meaning of the regulatory regime in the courts. Privatisation in the time frame and on the terms and conditions set in Fight Back is likely to complete the loss of national autonomy begun by the Hawke/Keating government when it abolished exchange controls in 1983. Consciously or not, there seems to be a bipartisan approach amongst the main parties in this election to the idea that ceding national autonomy to the play of international market forces is the necessary precondition for economic reform and success. I suspect that a lot of Australians are deeply disturbed by this attitude. Mr Keating, however, apparently believes voters can be distracted by superficial appeals to their innate nationalism by offering the prospect of a republic to replace the crown and changing the flag.'

I think that's quite interesting because what's the point of having a republic if your companies and everything aren't Australian?

HARRY: Well, it makes it easy for the flag, doesn't it, because with the share Britain has got we should leave their flag in the corner; with the share America's got of Australia we should put their flag in a corner, and put a United Nations one for some of the other bits and pieces. Singapore and Hong Kong are surprisingly large investors, so a share each for them. And we should put Japan, right in the centre because of its dominant position, and then we've got a flag that represents the ownership of Australia. I find this absolutely incredible.

You could have added Arnotts to that list you read out. What a tragedy that was! It was successful; they even had the money to buy out the Campbell's soup people but, of course, the government has this philosophy 'if we don't own the country it's good for us', something which is beyond most people.

What Ken Davidson alludes to there is the bipartisan approach, like other bipartisan approaches to issues in Australia which I've touched on before such as immigration, which just means that it's decided by our betters and nobody else gets a say.

HARRY: This is like a Canberra culture where everybody's gone to the same school, no matter which party. Certainly we've been highly critical of the Labor Party because they've been in power, but I don't think the Liberal/Nationals would have done much better. They never said boo about flogging off Arnotts.

What about 'working dog' biscuits?

A thought on the Arnotts' takeover. I use the phrase 'loss of ethos'. Ethos says it all . . . the spirit of the community, the spirit of the nation. And we get this spirit from ordinary things around us. It's not until they are taken away that we realise how important they are to us. Vegemite with an American accent isn't the same and neither will Arnotts' Bikkies be. It may be time to remind the bureaucrats and power politicians that every rule and piece of legislation is man-made and can just as easily be man-unmade. We just have to have the collective will to make it happen.

It's been said before that we Australians are a weird mob. We've laid down and let the Poms, the Yanks and now the Japanese colonise our country with their mighty currencies. Well, maybe we are weird enough to draw the line at the Teddy Bear biscuit. After all, some things are really worth fighting for . . . mate!

I've been sitting here staring at my computer screen, struggling with the 'man-made' bit. Person-made just didn't sound right and then it dawned on me. Yes, the rules might be man-made, but how about rallying the other force and getting them woman-unmade. I'll guarantee there are armies of women who are prepared to take up their scissors and cut the red tape to shreds. If we can't take a stand for a Teddy Bear we're not worth a packet of bikkies!

From: **Ann Orton, Mildura, Victoria**

T his is the story of a real Aussie battler, and of her attempt to do something about the falling prices and the falling demand for mohair and the coarser breeds of wool—WITHOUT government help, WITHOUT subsidies, WITHOUT using the taxpayers' money. Almost single-handedly, until a few days ago when a committee moved in to give a hand, she has promoted the idea of a 'Fleece Weekend', to teach two skills which require a lot of wool and mohair— the making of felt, and the making of wool and mohair fleece rugs.

The idea came up about three months ago, during a discussion about the difficulties of local growers who had bales of wool and mohair in their sheds, which had cost as much as ever to produce, but weren't worth sending away, and may not have fetched back the freight out. And the thought of slaughtering flocks which had been built up with care and well looked after for years was not on. So what to do?

A well-known visiting teacher of weaving, Ann Greenwood, suggested that mohair and the coarser breeds of wool made great fleece rugs, and away it went from there.

In the district were two craftswomen who made excellent felt and others skilled in the use of chemical and natural dyes. The teacher of weaving was enthusiastic about the idea of teaching the rug-making, and a well-known arts marketing consultant offered to lead a 'think tank' on ways and means to market these and other handmade products.

Yesterday twenty people arrived at a health retreat outside Buchan to learn to make the rugs, and another ten to join the felting class. This morning another twenty will arrive, plus twenty more adults and ten children to join the felting workshops. Fifty people in all, learning skills which, by their very nature, will create a market for the fleece the Japanese don't want—at least, not at the sort of prices which will keep the growers in business.

And behind it all? A quiet, rather shy, grey-haired lady, who will also be sitting at a loom, learning to make the rugs.

Her name is Beth. About ten years ago her home, representing a lifetime of saving from wages, was entered in her absence and fired. She lost everything—clothing, bedding, a lifetime collection of books and pictures—even the insurance. Since then she has been living in a caravan without electricity, without plumbing, without an indoor toilet or the amenities most of us consider 'normal'. She was sixty at the time, and with the sale of eggs, and milk from her house cow, and the money she got from the land on which her home once stood she started again—working and saving towards owning a home again.

Last year she was almost there (for a very small cottage) but the money saved from her pension, from work, from self-denial and from her land was invested in Pyramid. And that was that!

But was that the end? Knocked down for good? No sir! This is the story of the true Aussie old-timer spirit! She's up and fighting back again—this time for the 'Fleece Weekend'. Single-handedly, she has delivered forty bags of fleece around Gippsland to centres near Nowa Nowa, Lake Tyers, Lakes Entrance, Bairnsdale, Briagalong, Buchan—and people booked into the workshops and local craft groups have scoured and washed them. The whole complicated business of handling six separate workshops, running concurrently during one residential weekend, has been thought through and handled by her on her old-fashioned typewriter in her 'spare' time.

She isn't a comfortably off 'retired' person with time on her hands. She's usually out in a paddock—hand-feeding the cows she hand-reared as an investment towards the home she dreamed about, or feeding the chooks, or digging the garden, or slashing the blackberry. You name it!

A lot of old-timers like her listen to *Australia All Over*, Ian. They'd understand.

Joan, Jane and some of the folks at W-Tree and Buchan, Victoria

IAN TALKS WITH FRED SYKES

FRED: I've got a company called Emu Sporting Products here in Brisbane and I'm the only manufacturer of all-weather footballs in Australia. It's been a two-year project for us and we're now in our eleventh week of manufacturing.

Just to give you an idea, we are supposed to be the greatest sporting nation in the world for Rugby League and Rugby Union, but 728,286 Rugby League, Rugby Union and Australian Rules balls were imported from India last year. Can you believe it?

No, I can't believe it. Don't tell me they don't buy yours—what's the story?

FRED: We're finding it a little bit hard at the moment. Our balls are far superior and I think just about every Australian knows what's going on with quality and so forth from the overseas companies. It's a bit of a shame that Australians and the federal government aren't really backing the manufacturing sector. For instance, just recently the federal government bought 4000 imported balls. I went for the tender and because they were a couple of dollars cheaper than me, even though my quality's far superior, they decided to go for the Indian balls.

All the balls are made in India? Isn't it amazing!

FRED: A firm in Victoria makes the leather balls for the top games of the VFL, but their synthetic stuff is all fully imported.

Well, I don't know what to say, Fred, except the tail's wagging the dog.

FRED: Yes, it's all upside down.

Especially when we've got a million people or more out of work, it seems a bit funny, doesn't it? How many could you employ if you were making 750 000 more balls than you are now?

FRED: Well, we're going for the New South Wales and the Queensland Rugby League contracts this year. The official ball for the NSW Rugby League is imported from India as well, but I could go from six people to sixty if I get that contract.

Well, good luck, mate. It would be nice if an Australian company was making our own footie balls for whatever code.

It is hard to sympathise with my wool-growing friends, as they have been amongst the most vocal in advocating the need for a free market, and the removal of industry protection has hurt farmers more than any other industry.

When I was young people were paid to go around the paddocks collecting what was called 'dead wool', wool from dead sheep. In that period we processed our own wool. Remnants of the old scour works are still visible in many places. These removed the foreign matter and yolk from the wool.

Wool was in everyone's home and on everyone's back. The mothers in even the poorest of families spent many long hours knitting. Our wool is now processed overseas; a monopoly has been created. The price of wool in Australia has been pushed down and the profits remain overseas.

The only avenue open to Australia is to create a scarcity. The wool stockpile should be waterproofed and dumped in the sea, to save the storage costs, and be collected at a later date.

The money saved should be spent on creating a co-operative, to process the wool, turn it into garments, consumer products. We would get a cheaper product, the wool growers would make more money, and everyone would be happy, except the overseas monopolies.

From: Glenn Bradley, Bowraville, New South Wales

I suggest those who are concerned about lack of Australian-made goods in our stores should voice their complaints in writing.

I wrote to a leading store expressing disappointment that, at a time of a wool crisis, they were stocking scarcely any jumpers made in Australia. I explained I was even prepared to pay more for our own products and would not buy garments from overseas under the present circumstances.

I pointed out I had no criticism of the service offered by the sales staff, but only of store policy. In reply the manager said the situation was under review and that he had passed on my letter to those responsible for stock buying.

It was obvious from the tone of his letter that complaints such as mine must now be sufficient in number to make the store take notice.

So my advice to like-minded people is START WRITING!

From: Hal Brier, Fig Tree Pocket, Queensland

I heard a caller saying wool was too expensive to buy for ordinary people. Please publicise the fact that it is NOT. At the recent Wool Day in Perth's Hay Street Mall I saw a fashion parade of wool and wool blend garments from an

Australia-wide chain store priced from $50 and up, the most expensive being an exclusive patterned hand knit for $150. The garments were beautifully made, fashionable wear for day through to evening including skirts, pants, jackets and jumpers and cardigans—modelled by young people, but very wearable for any age. And, at $50 or $60, cheaper than a lot of other fabric items.

A large man's jumper can be made in pure new machine-washable Patons wool for less than $30. Soft and beautiful to touch and wear. I'm sure these garments and knitting wool are available in many other places.

From: Mrs Wendy Anderson, Kojonup, Western Australia

I couldn't believe my eyes when I saw a display of a particular brand of wool, in Launceston. There is nothing wrong with it—the price is the same as Patons—but it comes from England. Can you understand it? I can't . . . words fail me.

From: Jane Stark, West Tamar, Tasmania

I am the proprietor of a small local haberdashery/crystal/craft shop and in the past seven years I have sold wool on request, purely because of the cost involved in having every colour and type sitting on the shelves. I have shown my customers the wool colour and ply chart; they have selected the colour and type of wool they desired and I purchased this in from the wholesaler. This year, however, I became extremely frustrated when I learnt that the colour charts I have are now out of date, and there are no current charts available to me (probably because I have small orders).

As it is impossible to describe colours over the phone I am unable to supply this service to my customers any longer, which forces them to go to the larger monopolies and shopping centres many kilometres from their homes—in their cars, of course—to purchase their wool, if available, or, if not, jumpers made in China.

This, to me, is a very good example of wool companies not being serious about trying to sell as much wool as possible in every outlet available, and the poor service they provide. It is time they realised that people do still want to shop in small shops in comfort, where they can choose knitting patterns and wool in a relaxed atmosphere: customers are customers no matter where they purchase their wool.

From: Coral Serisier, Oatley, New South Wales

WHAT SHALL WE DO WITH THE WOOL?

We could knit lots of jumpers,
And socks, and scarves, and gloves;
And teddy bear hand puppets,
Which every small child loves.
We could all buy new carpet,
Made out of wool, of course;
And crochet brilliant blankets,
For our picnics (or our horse)
We could use cosy lambskin
To make up cuddly toys
Which are so very comforting
To tiny girls and boys
We could knit for Somalia
That most unhappy land
They deserve some comfort
And we could lend a hand.
We could use wool for making hats
To keep off rain or sun;
There's no end to the ideas
One thinks of, once begun.
But my last suggestion
Just may cause some surprise:
Give it all to our MPs
To pull over our eyes
So when they're misbehaving
And spouting lots of bull
It will be quite easy then
For them to 'pull the wool'

But I've got fur...

From: **Helen Brumby, Rose Bay, Tasmania**

To me it seems ironic to be encouraging people to buy Australian made or from Australian companies when the Federal and State governments are selling off Australian land and assets as fast as they can, and with no prior consultation with the Australian people. Our most dependable income earners are being flogged off without our permission and now the politicians are wondering why the balance of payments is tipping the wrong way. What is the point of

51

buying a pair of woollen socks when the whole country is being sold out from underneath us?

As to buying wool—what a joke! The wool board is not interested in selling unless it can shift the stuff by the container-load and for unrealistic prices. They fail to realise that the whole world knows about the massive wool surplus and, while it exists, will not be so dumb as to offer the sorts of prices the wool board is demanding. Yet when enterprising and innovative Australians, with excellent new ideas about uses for wool, approach the board to buy a few bales at a time, they're stonewalled.

Many people are willing to buy Australian wool products, if only they could find any. In response to the plight of the woolgrowers I heard that someone tried to get their offices carpeted with Australian wool carpet, but apparently no such thing exists. You can buy woollen products, but they are all made in Italy or France or somewhere else.

Not only does it seem impossible to buy raw wool in small quantities and who knows, maybe even save the industry, but, even if it *were* possible, it seems there are no facilities available to wash the wool!

I have no idea how to get out of the mess we are in; I suspect a fundamental change in government and corporate thinking has to come about—that is that mass production, mass this and mass that have to make some room for individual and small-scale enterprise and effort. Instead of mass conformity there has to come a dawning of a sense of individual cooperation as a business ethic. Or would that require too much individual integrity?

From: Ilona Roberts, North Tamborine, Queensland

I live in the Eastern Riverina and by nature am an incurable optimist. I would like you to pass on some of the following points I have noticed in my forty years' experience on the land.

In 1971 wool was worth about thirty cents per pound and the economists said there was no reason for wool to ever go much higher. In 1972 wool was worth four times the price and the best information I could get was that China wanted wool and bartered with Japan to come and buy it for them.

To the bureaucrats who say we have over-produced wool: how many people realise that we sold about one and a half million kilograms more wool than we grew this last season. Each local merino breeder I know is planning to sell his last year's wether lambs to the butcher, which will also contribute to a very severe shortage of woolgrowing sheep when the season eventually returns to normal.

So to all those battling drought and low wool price—hang on in there if you possibly can, as I believe the turnaround will come sooner than a lot of people think.

As far as the Australian economy is concerned I am firmly convinced that there is no possible way in this whole wide wonderful world that a recovery can occur until the rural community is returned to prosperity.

From: Mervyn Dehnert, Walbundrie, New South Wales

IAN TALKS WITH RAY WAYGOOD

RAY: Since March this year we've been carting live emus from Perth to the eastern states for a breeding program. I've invented a two-deck emu crate that carts eighty adult birds in one load or 400 chickens or 100 yearlings.

The market for emus is expanding all the time, isn't it?

RAY: That's right. They started breeding them in 1985 on an Aboriginal farm in Wiluna in Western Australia. Over here they're just breeding them up for the time being, but when they start slaughtering they use the emus for oil and meat processing to export overseas.

Tell us about the crate you carry them in.

RAY: It's similar to a two-deck cattle crate and we load underneath with general freight going to Perth—we put twenty pallets of general freight on the bottom deck and two or three motor cars on the top. When we get to Perth we off-load that and re-load with emus.

What are they like to carry? Are they docile?

RAY: No, they're very wild. They've been domestically bred through incubation but it hasn't bred the bad streak out of them. You have to catch the blighters individually to load them and they kick like buggery; it's a pretty slow process.

Well, I suppose we'd be the same, mate! How do you catch them—do you put a lasso around their neck?

53

RAY: No, you have to put your arm around their neck and pull them into your body and walk them straight up onto the loading ramp. They peck, too. They're very inquisitive animals; you daren't wear shoes with laces because they'll try to peck them off.

How did you get involved, Ray?

RAY: I've been taking general freight to Perth for twenty-eight years. When Victoria came into line with a wild-life licence I was asked would I bring a load of emus over. I thought they meant twenty pallets of Emu grog! So we brought twenty-four breeding emus across in March and it's been going strong ever since. There are forty-eight emu farms in Western Australia. One property we're carting from up near Meekatharra farms 11 000 emus—they've got 2000 breeders and this year they had 9000 chicks.

Do you go up to Meekatharra, then down to Perth and across the Nullabor to Yarrawonga?

RAY: To Yarrawonga, Leongatha, Korumburra, right through the South Gippsland area—4000 kilometres for each load of emus. We fill old car tyres with water so it won't splash out and just throw grain on the deck every four or five hours so they can have a bit of a feed. They like people making conversation with them so you talk to them all the time.

There's obviously a big market for them overseas.

RAY: I recently went to a conference in Perth. There were 300 delegates from all over the world, America, France, New Zealand . . . they've got 60 000 emus in Texas. It looks like it's going to be a big industry here in Australia.

I just hope I'm in first class...

COUNTRY CAFES
BREAKFAST 1/6d

This Greek cafe story came out of a 'weather' call from George Pope of Blaxland, New South Wales:

I was born in 1931 in Barellan, which is near Griffith, NSW, in the middle of a heatwave. It hadn't been under 100° for four days. My mother had had a long labour and was rather distressed and my grandmother came down the paddock where Dad was stripping his wheat to tell him that I'd been born. He abandoned stripping wheat for the day and headed for the hospital, but his first stop was Angelo Roufogalis's cafe. Angelo and Dad were great friends and knowing that Mum was in hospital without an electric fan he asked Angelo if he could buy a tray of ice blocks. He took it to the little cottage hospital and my mother always said that it was the most thoughtful and best present he gave her in fifty years of married life. She was able to wrap the ice blocks in face flannels, sponge her body with them to cool herself down and suck the rest!

Most of the wonderful Greek cafes have disappeared and nowadays we Aussies mostly eat in road houses outside of town. I might open a cafe with Hector and George Conomos and use the old Barwon Cafe menu. Will you come?

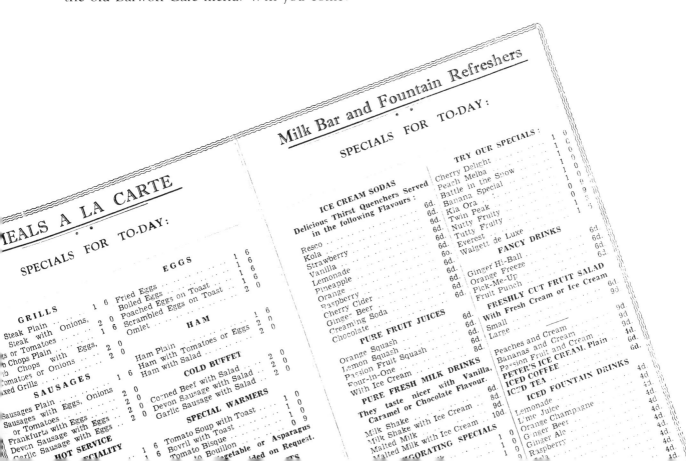

The Barwon Cafe
Walgett
—o—

MENU

CONOMOS BROS., Proprietors

P.O. BOX 61   PHONE 59

" LUXURY " THEATRE

ICE WORKS

WINE SALOON

CORDIAL FACTORY

Agencies—ANGUS & COOTE JEWELLERY
TEXACO MOTOR SPIRIT & OILS
PETERS' FAMOUS ICE CREAM

Thought you might be interested in the 'Cocky Conomos' Goes West story. Let me give a short background. My father, Hector Conomos, is one of the Conomos Brothers referred to in the cockatoo story. He is eighty-nine years young living at Randwick in Sydney. In his retirement he spends much time rummaging through documents, clippings and other nostalgic bits of paper he saved during his hard-working years as a businessman in Walgett. Dad went to Walgett in 1917 as a lad of fifteen and left in 1974 to live at Randwick.

You no doubt know Conomos isn't exactly Anglo-Saxon. The old Greek country cafe was an integral and vital part of many country towns in New South Wales and Queensland (and probably other states). The majority of the New South Wales cafes were owned and operated by Greeks who came from the little island of Kythera. In our part of New South Wales, for example, the cafes in Walgett, Carinda, Collarenabri and Goodooga were all once run by Kytherians who provided a terrific service to the townfolk, graziers, commercial travellers and visitors to their towns. Many of your 'older' listeners would relate to the Greek cafe.

'COCKY CONOMOS' GOES WEST

Many visitors to Walgett, as well as local and district people, will be sorry to hear of the demise of 'Cocky Conomos'. This white cockatoo has been at the Barwon Cafe for the past sixteen years and was known far and wide for his many tricks. He was admired by everybody and indeed Mr Conomos has often been offered a big price for the bird. But, as Lambros always said—money could not buy him.

We understand an employee was moving the truck out of the back yard and we believe the bird had a habit of shamming to bite the tyre as the truck started off. This day, however, he must have put his head too far under the wheel, which went over it and crushed it.

Naturally Conomos Bros were some-what upset at losing such a valuable bird.

From the Walgett *Spectator* of 4th December, 1946.

From: George Conomos, Longueville, New South Wales

I was transported back to my hometown when you interviewed Hector and George Conomos.

I was born and grew up in Walgett and knew Hector, his children, Helen, George and Nina well. Hector sounded the same as ever and I could just picture his smile. The Barwon Cafe was an oasis where we met after school and on weekends, to talk and court. I was surprised that no one mentioned (or perhaps I missed it) the Luxury Theatre that Hector owned.

It was a beautiful two-storey white building with the name 'Luxury Theatre' written in gold. The seats and curtains were velvet; the usherettes wore long gold satin frocks. On special occasions we were taken to the pictures and sat 'upstairs'. As we grew older we sat 'downstairs' with our friends and Hector used to patrol the aisles with a flashing torch to check we behaved ourselves!

From: Judy Kenyon, Blackheath, New South Wales

Your talk with Hector and George Conomos was a real memory stirrer. During the late 'forties and early 'fifties we went back and forth between Goomeri and Hervey Bay a lot, and a diversion through Gympie to have lunch at Conomos' cafe was an infrequent but well-remembered treat. Goomeri had two Greek cafes of its own, one owned by Tony Argery, who was a shooting mate of my grandfather's and had a son, John, my age. There were two other Johns in our primary school class of eight, so he used the Greek form, Yani, and the other three of us became John, Johnnie and Johnno.

The other Greek cafe owner was Jimmy Black—obviously anglicised—a very kind and gentle man. Going in for a meal with a recently broken arm still in plaster I found myself whisked out to the kitchen and plonked down at a scrubbed wooden workbench beside his enormous wood stove. He cut up my meal and made sure I ate every scrap, in between making up meals for a dozen or so diners outside. And the smells—cafes don't smell the same now! Neither do grocery stores. Suspect it might have something to do with all the pre-processing and packaging. Same applies to taste. Milkshakes had a different taste when the milk came straight out of a cow that morning. Wasn't always an advantage. On one occasion a couple of cafe cows wandered into the yard behind my father's produce shed where we were picking over onions. They proceeded to eat the discards which suited us as it saved us having to dump them. But the milkshakes weren't up to their usual standard for a few days!

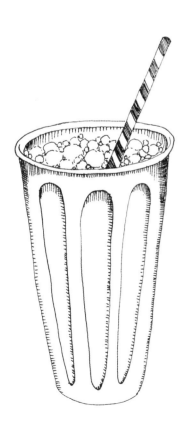

From: John Bourne, Thangool, Queensland

Listening to you talking to Hector Conomos on Sunday morning about his days in the cafe at Walgett brought back lots of memories and tears to my eyes. They were great people, 'the country Greeks'. I lived in Kyogle on the north coast in the 1930s and 1940s and my father had a shoe store next door to the best Greek cafe in country New South Wales. It had two sides to sit down—

'the ladies' side'—very posh, and 'the men's side'—still with marble-top tables, but a little more basic; the finest milk bar and soda bar you have ever seen; a cake counter; a vegetable section; a special chocolate counter and the general lolly and cigarette counter.

Partners, Stan and Peter, brought young boys out from Kythera to learn the business and Peter brought his wife out when he was about forty-five and my father taught her to speak English. They cooked their own cakes and pies and made their own ice cream. The waitresses in nice uniforms used to yell out on arrival in the kitchen 'one single' or 'one double'. A single was one meat pie with potato and gravy and a double, of course, was two meat pies. They were an institution in country towns and today's country towns are the worse off without them.

I write from Walgett, home of the Barwon Cafe and heart of Wolseley Country.
I have thoroughly enjoyed listening to the gems about our Barwon Cafe. My memories only relate to the mid-'fifties when I transferred to Walgett as a telephonist from the far north coast and lived at the local boarding house. Mealtimes at the boarding house did not always suit our hours of shift work and I often indulged at the Barwon. Meat pie with 'yummy' gravy was great value and, when the budget allowed, a banana split. I could always ask for more flavouring at no charge.

It was a 'people' cafe. The Conomos were astute business operators but their interest in their customers, locals or visitors, was simply great, warm and genuine.

I heard the little snippet of the Buffet Girls and it reminded me of my teenage years. In 1939 my parents opened a Milk Bar Cafe in a little town called Casterton in the Western District of Victoria. They called it 'The Henty' as the main street was called Henty Street after the original settlers who settled the district.

Anyway, my father, who was the son of an Italian migrant who had run away from school in Ballarat to enlist in the First World War, joined the Army as an Instructor at the beginning of the Second World War. This left my mother and her loyal girls to run the shop. In about 1943, I think, Ansett had the contract to move troops from the rail at Hamilton to camp at Mount Gambier and huge semi-trailer buses were used. They had a hostess on board and my mother organised a

Buffet stop at Casterton which was about halfway to Mount Gambier.

The hostess would take the orders and ring them from a village called Coleraine about twenty miles from Casterton. There was a great panic to cook steak and eggs, eggs on toast, toasted sandwiches that had been ordered for up to seventy men.

One day we had a convoy of American Marines go through and they all poured into our cafe demanding 'hot biscuits' and coffee. My mother had made dozens of hot scones that morning, but they hated our coffee—which was pretty awful as I remember!

From: Annette Proposeh, Rye, Victoria

Probably the most famous corner cafe in Wagga during the 'sixties was the Golden Gate. It wasn't actually on a corner but rather at the junction of Wagga's two main streets, just north of Wollundry lagoon. At the time it was run by the Spyros family, most notably Jerry and his son Johnny. Jerry drove a huge two-door convertible, metallic blue, Chevy Bison, or maybe it was a Pontiac Grizzly—I can't recall! All I know is that it was the only model of its kind in Wagga.

Johnny was a couple of years behind me and my friends at Wagga High School. I remember he found school a bit of a battle, due mainly to the general lack of understanding or support typical of Australian high schools of the time for people of non-British ancestry. The standing joke was that although his school maths was hopeless, his cafe maths was pure genius!

The thing that set Johnny apart from anyone else running an eatery was his 'Steaka sandwich justa fried onions and da gravy'. Every Sunday afternoon we would take over the back cubicles of the Golden Gate because we knew Johnny would be working the weekend and he knew exactly what we wanted. Anywhere from two to a dozen steak sandwiches, along with a couple of plates of chips and tomato sauce would be whipped up by Johnny, depending on how many of us turned up. It didn't matter how long we hung around afterwards because this was our place to meet, away from school and home. On the rare occasions when another family member worked Sundays we still ordered the usual, but it somehow lacked Johnny's special touch.

When we inevitably went our separate ways I left Wagga and never got back to the Golden Gate. These days I live in Newtown in Sydney and would you believe Jerry is running a petrol station on Enmore Road!

From: Keith Wilson, Newtown, New South Wales

As a small child growing up in Balranald I recall the Royal Cafe in Market Street. The cafe was run by a big Greek man called Greg Condos. It was a large cafe with lots of tables and chairs that always seemed to have people sitting at them.

Greg to me was a big happy man and his family were great people. It didn't matter how little change one had you could always buy something. Banana splits were out of this world!!

The local picture theatre was next door and each Saturday night after the flick the cafe would be full to capacity with the locals having supper—anything from toasted sangos to mixed grills.

Those were the days! Nothing was a trouble to these wonderful people.

From: **Decca and Ellen Duryea, Maude, New South Wales**

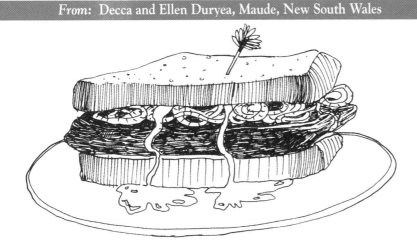

IAN TALKS WITH DICK KELSH

You're a truckie, are you, Dick?

DICK: I suppose you'd call me a born-again truckie! I used to be a truckie until the economic conditions back then got the better of us and I went fencing contracting. I spoke to you once before about our electric dingo fence we built years ago. I did that for quite a number of years and we're back in the trucks now.

What are you doing at the moment?

DICK: We've got a pretty hot load of freight on, actually. In fact, I reckon at the moment we hold the balance of power in the next federal election.

Why's that, mate?

DICK: We've got all the ballot boxes for Western Australia on board, so we might pull up at the border and ring old Keating up and tell him to pull his horns in and let us have a fair go!

Oh, that's a bit rough, mate. Do you deliver the ballot boxes to one place or do you drop them off all over the place?

DICK: I wish we could drop them off all over the place, but we leave them with Comet in Perth and they'll distribute them.

How many boxes are there?

DICK: I've got no idea. There are about twenty pallets on each truck, so there's a fair few of them. They're folded down and have to be put together when we get over there.

Have you been driving for a fair while this morning?

DICK: Oh, no, we only drive for five hours at a time and then we knock off for a break.

So you're in Port Augusta now. When will you get to Perth?

DICK: Don't tell anybody, but we're supposed to be there tomorrow morning! Just another thing—I don't know whether many people take notice of the regrowth of native trees across Australia but in the last eighteen months the regrowth is absolutely staggering.

In any particular area?

DICK: Well, from where the treeline starts this side of the Nullarbor right through to Port Augusta you couldn't count the little quandong trees. And we were north of Griffith the other day and native pine there has come up so thickly you could never walk through it if it develops. It's not because of big rains because they started to grow before the heavy rain started, so I think old nature knows what it's doing.

Well, thanks for calling us this morning and look after those ballot boxes.

LAND AND SKY

You'll come across a page of photographs in here that show something of this unique continent's hazards, beauty and sheer vastness. Imagine being an explorer such as Ernest Giles in the 1870s, battling the interior with relatively primitive equipment and supplies. Even in our four-wheel-drive 1990s we are fully challenged by Outback conditions.

As this book reaches its final stages of production the wattles are coming into bloom. So the following two verses from a poem, The Early Wattle, written by C Company, Victoria and published in *The Australian Woman's Mirror*, August 26, 1941, seem very appropriate. The full poem is reproduced in this chapter.

If all that sunset-coloured sky
Were gathered into gold
And looped on branches low or high
Your story might be told

From some far landscape battle-scarred
'Mid war's foul disarray
The glory of my own land, starred
With wattle bloom today

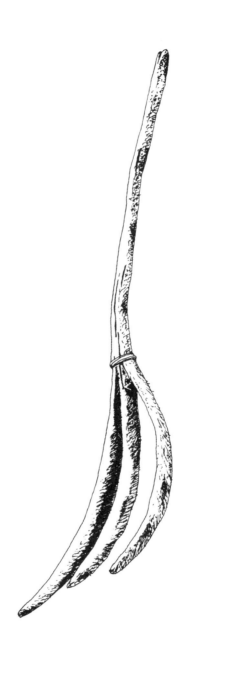

Western Myall is the wattle (*Acacia papyrocarpa*) which is spotted through a lot of salt bush in big areas of rangeland, eg north of the Nullarbor. The present trees are old; new ones rarely grow. Carolyn Ireland researched the seeding (she had a grant from the Australian Flora Foundation). Ants run away with most of the seed. Her theory is that a big storm or two is needed just after seeding (before the ants get to the seed) for success in germination.

It would be nice to hear from people who worked on sheep stations there decades ago, to see if they can remember a special year when lots of myall saplings got going.

From: Malcolm Reed, President, Australian Flora Foundation Inc, New South Wales

I thought you would enjoy making the golden wattle pancakes on Wattle Day. We have them each year and enjoy them. The larger pompoms on the golden wattle are the easiest to pick, although any wattle would do, except it is very arduous to get two cups of the smaller softer blooms.

Golden Wattle Pancakes

Beat together two egg yolks and one ounce of melted butter, add half a cup of milk, half a cup of flour and two cups of golden wattle flowers (stems removed). Mix well and lastly fold in stiffly beaten egg whites. Drop spoonfuls into buttered pan and fry like pancakes. They are nice and have a nutty flavour.

From: Bess Larkins, Lake Tyers Beach, Victoria

Woodlands and grasslands dominated by kangaroo grass, or *Themeda australis*, were originally very common over much of Australia, including the south east. It is not clear exactly why this summer growing grass was so widespread in predominantly winter rainfall zones but it certainly had something to do with regular burning. Remove the burning and the kangaroo grass usually disappears and invasion by introduced grasses and weeds follows with subsequent loss of the other native species.

Steam engines used to give off quite a lot of sparks which were often responsible for starting bushfires. To minimise the danger, crews continually burnt off the grass beside the railway lines, usually in spring and autumn, and the railway reserves were often ribbons of grassland and grassy woodland dominated by kangaroo grass and containing many small but spectacular flowers and a fascinating array of other native grasses. The regular burning was essential for the survival of these interesting and important plant communities.

The passing of the steam trains meant that the regular burning ceased and these grasslands have mostly been invaded by introduced grasses and weeds. We have therefore lost these ribbons of native grasslands, although their passing has not attracted nearly as much attention as the destruction of rainforests. All that is left in Tasmania and Southern Victoria are tiny remnants and these are mostly on the way out. I recently attended a workshop in Melbourne attended by about thirty grassland scientists from southern Australia concerned with the preservation of these tiny remnants, particularly those dominated by kangaroo grass and the reconstruction of more examples of them for future generations.

Who would have thought that the passing of the steam trains would lead, indirectly, to the almost complete loss of important remnant vegetation in parts of Victoria and Tasmania?

From: Wal Whalley, Botany Department, University of New England, New South Wales

Most people will know that James Cook was the first to chart the eastern seaboard of Australia and to map New Zealand (that is, he surveyed them), but do you know what the first aim of his initial trip to the Pacific was?

Cook's primary instruction was to observe the passage of the planet Venus across the face of the Sun in 1769. That expedition was sent at great expense since by getting accurate timing of the transit time (such a thing occurs in pairs eight years apart about every century) it was thought that the distance from the Earth to the Sun could be accurately determined, and that would lead to better navigation tables. Cook and his team observed the transit successfully from Tahiti and then explored our part of the world. However—and here's the rub—the observations of the transit were of no use ultimately since an effect due to the bending of light in the terrestrial atmosphere caused an uncertainty in the Earth–Sun distance which had not been anticipated by the scientists involved. Prominent amongst these was Sir Edmund Halley, he of the comet.

So was Cook's voyage a failure, given that Australia would not be in the same thriving state now if he had not been sent to view Venus from the South Pacific? Of course my message here is quite self-serving: people moan about money being spent on seemingly abstract scientific research with no economic benefit, but quite apart from its educational value, very often enormous benefits arise which had never been imagined, indeed were not even imaginable, in the first place. Do you think that the physicists who invented the laser were thinking of compact disks or supermarket scanners back in the late 1950s?

I cannot leave you without saying when the next transit of Venus will occur, so that you can make a date in your diary. The great day will be the eighth of June in 2004, and yes you will be able to see it from Australia. If it's cloudy that day then you'll need to wait until the sixth of June 2012, with Australians again being able to spot Venus silhouetted against the fiery orb of the Sun.

From: Dr Duncan I. Steel, Anglo-Australian Observatory, Coonabarabran, New South Wales

THE EARLY WATTLE

If all that sunset-coloured sky
Were gathered into gold
And looped on branches low or high
Your story might be told

If Solomon's lost treasure might
Be found again and flung
Along the valley ridge tonight
Your beauty might be sung

Oh, fragrance on the evening breeze,
Oh, magpies' vesper call
I wonder, warring overseas,
How often I'll recall

From some far landscape battle-scarred
'Mid war's foul disarray
The glory of my own land, starred
With wattle bloom today

Published in *The Australian Woman's Mirror*, Vol 17 No 40, August 26, 1941

From: C. Company, Victoria

On your program the question was asked—'How far north is the Southern Cross visible?'

Back in antiquity, around 2000 BC, the Cross was visible from the Mediterranean, but at present can be seen only from the Southern Hemisphere. This was due mainly to the way all the stars in our galaxy are rotating around its centre, all at different speeds. The Sun and planets are situated about three quarters of the way out from the centre towards the outer rim and are orbiting at a speed of 225K per second. Over time this has the effect of determining the position of stars in relation to each other and they are seen from a different perspective. According to Hoyle, we (the Sun and planets) pass stars on our outside, and are being passed by stars on the inside. Even at the seemingly fast speed of 225K per second it takes the Sun and planets 200 million years to make one circuit of the galaxy. There are an estimated ten thousand million other galaxies: we are small fry indeed.

From: Keith Gallagher, Lawrence, New South Wales

My wife and I heard the discussions about the Latin phrase *OB TERRAS RECLUSAS* following your Coolgardie program, when you first told of it being inscribed on the gravestone of the explorer, Ernest Giles.

Ob is a Latin preposition which will translate such English phrases as 'on account of, because of, for the sake of, in consideration of, as recompense for, by reason of'.

Terras is the form of the plural required after the preposition *ob*. It means in this context 'lands, regions, tracts, territories'.

Reclusas is one of the participles from the verb *recludo, recludere, reclusi, reclusum*, 'to unclose, throw open, disclose, reveal, expose'.

Putting this together, then, we have a very literal translation: 'In consideration of lands having been revealed or discovered'—the headstone is a memorial erected 'in honour of his explorations and the lands opened up as a result'. What an appropriate epitaph to Ernest Giles!

From: Jim Stoodley, Mt Gravatt, Queensland

You were asking last week about the meaning of *ob terras reclusas*. *Terras reclusas* means 'lands that have been opened up'. The '*ob*' can mean various things, but it probably means 'for the sake of . . .' Does this fit the context? I did not hear how it was that you came across it.

Sunday morning is a busy time for me, so I don't get much chance to listen to

Australia All Over, but what I do hear is a delight. As you said the other day, those beautiful old voices! The Australian voice is like a wine of strong character—a bit rough at first, but mellowing into something beautiful.

From: Fr Bill David, Jesuit Theological College, Parkville, Victoria

L iterally '*terra reclusas*' says 'to open the earth'—*terra* means earth and *reclusas* is Latin for 'to open'. So perhaps this would have recorded the deeds of a miner—appropriate for Coolgardie, I feel.

From: Betty Cove, Moe, Victoria

I was never much good at Latin. Used to get 'the cuts' once every day at school for Latin, and twice on Thursdays. That's because we had two Latin periods on Thursdays.

But I have a friend who was pretty good. I asked him and got this suggestion.
'*ob*'—abbreviation of '*obit*' meaning 'he (or she) dies '*ob*' has a wide range of meanings, but they all carry the idea of finality.
'*terras*'—earth
'*reclusas*'—locked, away interred
'*ob terras reclusas*'—'finally buried in this earth' or more loosely 'buried here'

It suggests to me that, after all the hundreds and hundreds of miles Giles roamed through this great land of ours, in the end here he is confined to this small plot of earth.

From: Harry, a regular listener

'D aylight Saving' in my case represents 'Daylight Losing'. Each time it has come in here in recent years there have been letters in *The Advertiser* advocating that those who wish to finish work early (to get skin cancer these days perhaps) should simply start and finish work an hour earlier by standard time. This would avoid all the clock changing, hyperbole, argumentation, ballyhoo and, above all, inconvenience to the many of us who don't like it.

I got up earlier than usual this morning but on the clock it was later (lost time). Tonight I'll watch Channel 2 news in broad daylight when I could be doing other things.

Useful time lost morning and evening!

From: John Bull, Brighton, South Australia

Y ou were wondering about the origins of the name Capella. Ludwig Leichhardt passed through the area on his first successful and aborted second expedition and named the peaks that are seen from Capella after members of his first expedition.

Capella is a northern hemisphere bright red star that is seen low in the north sky from the town of Capella during the period Christmas to Easter. Early surveyors to the area who looked at the stars (no TV) named their camps after the prominent stars they observed.

The creek was first named Capella Creek and when coaches ran from Rockhampton to Copperfield (Clermont) a hotel/coach station was built by the waterhole on the creek and the site named Capella. In 1882 a town was surveyed at this site which became the township of Capella.

From: Andy Plunkett, Capella, Queensland

I have just returned home after driving around Australia on Highway One. I travelled in an anti-clockwise direction and am able to confirm that more tail winds are encountered by doing so. The only head winds I experienced were coming east from Western Australia, when I was unlucky enough to have strong head winds most of the way. Whereas I was averaging fourteen litres per hundred kilometres (or twenty miles per gallon) for most of the trip, for the two days I spent on the Nullarbor, head winds increased consumption to twenty litres per hundred kilometres or fourteen miles per gallon! This proved a worry, with the shortage of fuel stops, and meant slowing down to sixty kilometres per hour just to make sure I would not run out of petrol.

From: Ross Mackenzie, Dickson, Australian Capital Territory

J ust a few points taken from Oxford Dictionary.
'corrugate'—wrinkle, bend
'corrugations'—wavy ridges
I remember an old west coast farmer talking about his old Model 'T'—'just hanging to pieces and the coronations on the road shook his divorce pipe off'.

From: Kelly, Horsham, Victoria

M y father encountered corrugations often on the north coast line while driving a 'motor bike'. He was a mechanic for the NSWGR and was based at the South Grafton workshops. It was referred to as 'chattering'

because of the noise made by the wheels of rolling stock as they passed over it. The cause was 'wheel bounce' and it occurred mainly on the faster sections of track. A bouncing wheel would leave tiny indentations on the rail surface, which in turn caused other wheels to bounce, deepening the indentation and eventually forming ripples that would spread along the track. It was believed that the expansion gaps left at rail joints were the trigger and I recall clearly my father pointing out to me the ripples on the rail surface, often extending for a couple of metres either side of a rail joint. When the old 'quarter lengths' were replaced by continuous welded rail, chattering still occurred.

A possible explanation is that vibrations from the wheels travel along the rails, causing resonance which is affected by the same vibrations reflected upwards from the soil structure beneath the track. These combined vibrations would only have to cause a fast-moving wheel to move a fraction upwards and chattering would occur. There are sections of track—especially around Coffs Harbour—that are not subject to chattering. The railway at Coffs Harbour passes over soil that is coastal in origin, with a high sand content, and it is possible that these softer sub-soils either absorb or deflect downward vibrations rather than reflect them back upwards.

Incidentally, these sections of track produce a smooth, near silent ride and several drivers have confided in me saying that there were sections in which they could notch up the loco a little to make up lost time, without alerting the guard.

From: Kim Buckles, Mawson, Australian Capital Territory

I have a theory about the cause of corrugations on dirt roads. The suspension of a modern vehicle absorbs the impact of the wheel against a stone or pothole through the shock absorber. This upward movement causes energy to be stored in a compressed suspension. The shock absorber compresses readily but it retards the rebound of the suspension back to its level state. The mass of the vehicle remains unaffected more or less as it is designed to be. Although the shock absorber retards the downward return of the spring, this movement nevertheless causes a downward thrust against the road surface, accentuated by the weight of the vehicle. All this happens in a split second at speeds of, say, eight kilometres an hour. This downward rebound causes the road to be punched by the tyre, in fact pummelled. So after a stone or pothole is hit a ripple effect is created on the road surface by the dissipated energy of shock absorption.

This action is self-perpetuated by continuing traffic and the entire road lengthens into a washboard surface. Where there is a bend in the road and brakes are applied prior to the bend the effect is more pronounced because of increased weight transfer onto the front suspension.

You have proof of this theory on bitumen roads where you see the formation of a second pothole in line with a primary one and then the development of a chain of potholes.

From: Don Mason, Goolwa, South Australia

It seemed generally accepted that corrugations were caused by aerodynamics. That may be, but a simpler explanation is suction. There were no corrugations in the early days of motoring as tyres were too narrow. Solid rubber or steel tyres will not cause corrugations and it was not till the advent of balloon tyres in the 'twenties and 'thirties that road corrugations occurred.

From: John Schinckel, Kybybolite, South Australia

My uncle Arch once told me that corrugations in the road were caused by carpet snakes who always crossed at the same place, in line abreast formation. But I've never seen them doing it.

From: Bill Scott, Warwick, Queensland

I am in a dilemma. I soon am going to drive around Australia and have been wrestling with the problem of whether to go clockwise or anti-clockwise. The other night at the pub I raised the problem with my mate, Fair Dinkum, and he assures me it is better to travel the journey anti-clockwise for one big reason. He points out to me that the pacers at Harold Park for some strange reason race anti-clockwise, and it is a well-known fact that a horse one-out from the rail travels about four metres more than the horse on the rails. Fair Dinkum goes on to theorise that with the keep to the left rule on our roads it must follow that going around Australia in a clockwise direction, and keeping to the left, you are virtually travelling one-out from the rail. Fair Dinkum says this will translate to about 178 miles, and it will thus save me heaps of time, fuel and wear and tear if I go the other way.

My wife always reckons that I am a couple of miles short of a kilometre when it comes to judging distances, but I find it difficult to find that Fair Dinkum's figures are faulty.

Unless some of your listeners can convince me otherwise, Macca, I shall be travelling anti-clockwise.

From: Graeme Murphy, Regentville, New South Wales

GOIN' RIGHT AROUND

We have this most awful dilemma
Our knickers all knotted because
We just do not know the best way to go
To travel our way around Aus.
Should we pack up our bags and go eastward
Then follow the coastline up North?
Or would it be best if we headed West
And—sun on our backsides—set forth?
The tip from a bloke called Fair Dinkum
(An expert from some pub Outback)
Gives us this advice, 'Go anti-clockwise
It's shorter on the inside track!
Less wear and tear on your tyres, mate
Less fuel to get there, you'll find
Fellers with brains, cross the Nullarbor Plains
With prevailing winds blowing behind.'
Don't know much about inside running
Or advantages brought by the winds
But on the home straight, we'll appreciate
The direction the bloody earth spins!!!

From: Margaret Glendenning, Everton Upper, Victoria

The information given by Fair Dinkum concerning the difference between clockwise and anti-clockwise travel around Australia was in gross error. I think Fair Dinkum said the difference was about 178 kilometres. This is nowhere near the mark. The difference is in fact only about thirty or forty metres. All of Fair Dinkum's talk about fuel usage is nonsense!

The other argument about making use of the prevailing winds makes a lot of sense, but not the distance argument.

From: Gary Prime, Warragul, Victoria

Fair Dinkum had a valid argument that anti-clockwise would be shorter than clockwise, but his calculations are up the pole. The difference due to this factor would be in the range of twenty metres to one hundred metres, that is, less than 0.1 kilometres.

this way... no this way...

The length of the circuit is irrelevant, as is the number of twists and turns as, no matter what configuration one devises, after the basic need to turn through 360 degrees in the relevant direction to complete a circuit, all other left and right turns cancel out.

The significant factor is the separation between CW and ACW traffic lanes, specifically on the bends. None on a single lane road, but could be quite significant on a freeway with a wide intermediate strip. Not many of these though on a round Australia route.

When everything is boiled down, whatever road plans you devise, the difference between CW and ACW is the difference in circumference of two circles whose difference in radius is the separation of the traffic lanes. If we allow fifteen metres for this, then the formula is: Pi $\times$ (difference in diameters) = Pi $\times$ (2 $\times$ separation) = Pi $\times$ 2 $\times$ 15 = 94 metres. Less for corner cutters, of course, and most roads.

So, look to other reasons to decide which way round to go.

Your caller referring to prevailing winds had a valid consideration, especially for vehicles towing vans. Would make many dollars' difference in fuel consumption for the trip.

From: Alan Austin, Brookton, Western Australia

On the seventh of April 1984, my forty-ninth birthday, I set off from Melbourne by bicycle on an around-Australia solo, unaccompanied journey in an anti-clockwise direction. I returned to Melbourne on the seventeenth of December 1984. Out of 140 cycling days, eighty-nine were into absolutely vile headwinds. So there is the living agonizing proof that anti-clockwise is not the way to go if drivers want to save petrol; or at least not during the months April to December.

In spite of the misery of so much headwind, I fell in love with this beautiful country, especially the area between Townsville, Katherine, Halls Creek and Port Hedland. It was the delicious visual feast that sustained me on bad days.

From: Jill Hale, Sandy Bay, Tasmania

It was refreshing to listen to your caller who did not approve the renaming of a certain stringybark species as white mahogany.

That man, a timber cutter in Queensland, displayed obvious bush knowledge when he stated that regenerated trees do far better than planted eucalypts. And you can certainly claim a first for any segment of the major media in letting this simple fact go to air or print. Congratulations!

The Forestry Commission of New South Wales carried out extensive plantings on the south coast during the 1960s, particularly of the valuable hardwood, spotted gum. This was an attempt to establish spotted gum forests where they had not previously existed. These trees are mostly still growing today—stunted, crooked saplings which will never be of commercial value.

During the same period poles and mill logs have continued to regenerate in forests which have been selectively harvested.

From: Dennis Moore, Bateman's Bay, New South Wales

The day's so clear you can see a fly up a tree and it's got a crook back leg

IAN TALKS WITH RALPH READER

RALPH: There was a lot of nostalgia in your program from the Territory. Did you know that Hawker, one of the most prestigious suburbs here in Canberra, has all the streets named for cattle stations in the Northern Territory. There's Kurundi Place, Ambalindum Street, Elsey Street (from *We of the Never Never*), Florina Place, Andado Place. I don't think people in that suburb know that those names came from the Territory, and likewise I don't think many in the Territory know that the streets are named after their properties.

Isn't that interesting! You've been in the Territory, Ralph, at one time or another?

RALPH: Yes, a few times. You mentioned Finke. Well, I was staying on Palmer Valley Station which isn't far from Finke and Andado—although everything's far from everything else up there! They were taking a mob of cattle from Palmer Valley to the railway siding at Finke to load them for Adelaide, and the cattle had left early in the morning. I followed in a jeep with the manager—a chap called Tony Greatorex, who became very prominent in the Territory—and we caught up with them at just about dark. They'd settled the cattle down and the stockmen, all Aborigines, were sitting around the fire. The head stockman was a charismatic Aborigine named Widgetty Mick. He was stocky, with grey hair and a grey beard. He was a laid back, laconic man of few words and Jock greeted him warmly. He said, 'Well, Widgetty, how are you', and Widgetty said, 'Oh, boss, I'm not too good, I think another clean shirt'll see me out!' I'm a doctor and I've often thought of that statement. If only we could deliver our prognoses in that way so that if somebody asked, 'Well, how much longer have I got, Doc', we could say, 'Well, I think another clean shirt'll see you out!'

Widgetty Mick sounds like the sort of bloke it'd be nice to sit down and have a yak to; when the Aborigines say something it's worth listening to.

ASPECTS OF NATURE

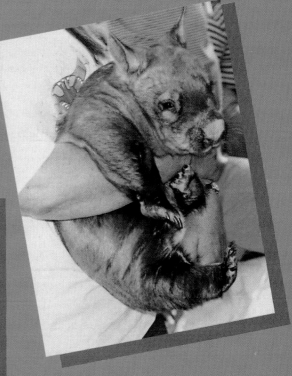

Some aspects of nature. A snake's life can be hazardous, particularly if it meets a bigger one. Look very closely and you'll see, below left, an albino emu and next to it emus in their regular colours.

Tina the wombat appears very snug in the arms of Prue Geddes from Warrawong Sanctuary in the Adelaide Hills; Ray Waygood looks on as emu passengers emerge from his two-deck cattle crate to stretch their legs.

LASSETER, EGG-BERT & GRAHAM

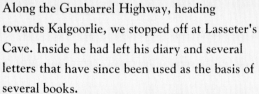

Along the Gunbarrel Highway, heading towards Kalgoorlie, we stopped off at Lasseter's Cave. Inside he had left his diary and several letters that have since been used as the basis of several books.

Question: How long have you been a truck driver?
Answer: I was a garbo and I suppose I got sick of running behind it; I wanted to drive it.
This is Graham from Windsor Gardens, shown at the picnic in Belair National Park in March 1994.

Egg-Bert the egg-eating goanna of Tumbulgum whose owner, Jan Sinclair, rang to describe the noises he makes.

A LITTLE BIT OF EVERYTHING

Sometimes I receive letters that just might offend someone. I don't want to offend anyone—well, not too often—so I don't read them on the program. But the book's the perfect place for such a letter. See how long it takes you to find it! Meantime, there are two early Christmas poems overleaf.

HOW I KNOW IT'S CHRISTMAS
Jessie Sandeman

The scent of frangipani tells us Christmas is near,
The red leaves on the mango trees come to farewell the year;
The early mangoes in the shops, the stone fruits blushing red
And watermelon, cold and sweet; the storm clouds overhead.
You probably have other ways of knowing Christmastime is here,
Visitors and letters, cards and festive cheer;
The smell of puddings steaming, or cakes about to burn
Will bring the memories all back, for childhood we may yearn.
For Sunday School and picnics and merriment and glee
With Santa Claus and jingling bells and perhaps a Christmas tree
The sights, the sounds the smell of Christmas
Stay all year round with me.

A MERRY CHRISTMAS
Bill Glasson

Where the western sky is shining with an all devouring heat,
And artesian bores are hot enough to cook a Swagman's meat;
Where for days a big Bedourie blots the sun out of the sky,
Where it hasn't rained for years and the river beds are dry;
Or it doesn't matter greatly if the rain is pouring down
And the 'ringers' are all pitching to the barmaids in the town
Where the Min Min Lights at sundown frighten those who chance to see
Sunday morning finds the locals listening to the ABC

Tales of steamers on the Murray brighten up our Sunday morn
Old-time shearers talk of tallies and the way the sheep were shorn
Coo-ee callers wake the echoes, lizard races stir the blood,
What about the bloke who sailed his tractor down a Murray flood.
'Why I live at Fanmacdangle' brings out some inspiring prose
But the time has come to bring the '86 Show to a close.
Go on home and make a hundred, Ian, the year has been grand,
And I wish a Merry Xmas to our McNamara's Band.

Over the past couple of weeks I have heard you and your listeners getting 'stuck into' the plastic five dollar note and I thought the following might change your mind, as it did mine.

As a teacher I took my grade to visit the Note Printing Works where these notes are printed and voiced my dislike for them to the tour guide. I was told that they are an all-Australian technology, using all-Australian products that are not only bringing in export dollars but are also recycled. The cotton variety, on the other hand, is made on 'paper' imported from Great Britain and burnt when no longer in circulation.

So you see the true 'feral fiver' is the paper one; the plastic one is Aussie through and through!

From: Dorothy Giusti, New Gisborne, Victoria

The speaker who felt that the feral five dollar note should be removed permanently seemed to be on the right track. It is time for STUFFD (Society To Undo Feral Five Dollars).

I am concerned, however, about the workload of your speaker in taking on personally the collection of all the Feral Five Dollars in Australia. It seems to me it would be better to have a representative in each state, and I am prepared to sacrifice my time collecting all FFDs sent to me. I will not, of course, be making a mint out of this project! What happens to them then could be decided by the Australian public (a first?).

Perhaps they could be glued to our wool stockpile, and recycled as a giant sculpture entitled 'Stuffed'?

From: Judi Cox, Kenmore, Queensland

I own and operate a supermarket in Brisbane. My staff and I handle all note and coin denominations in considerable volume. With few exceptions, transactions involving the plastic five-dollar note are accompanied with negative comments by the customers. Overwhelmingly this particular note is unpopular within the market place.

For those who use a purse or wallet, the following are some of the faults that I observe: invariably fall from the grip of the elderly; can easily be presented in twos or threes when one only is intended for presentation; once crumpled they won't reform to a flat note; don't store easily in a cash register drawer; won't lie in a flat pile during counting; difficult to count; they attract vandalism; they are not suitable for pocket storage (won't fold).

I'm sure a survey of the general public would endorse and add to my list of deficiencies.

From: Alec Francis, Rochedale, Queensland

THE CRAZY FIVE DOLLAR NOTE

Our five dollar note
Has become quite a curse
Won't fit without struggle
Into wallet or purse

Our prayer each day
As we kneel by the bed
Is not to get them in change
Or to find them instead
Enclosed with our hard-earned 'bread'

It curls up without touch
Can take off in swift flight!
Whither it goes——
It's no common old kite!

A man is left wondering
Who invented the note?
To penalise citizens
Minus query or vote?

They cannot be crushed
Or rolled into a ball
While waiting for stamps
Or working a stall

The note has an inkling
It's not real or fair go!
The place for it really
Is into the Po! (River that is?)

From: S. Powter, Fernvale, Queensland

IAN TALKS WITH MARGARET ELFORD

MARGARET: Ian, I wanted to talk to you about those 'feral fivers'—those plastic notes. I heard a letter being read out this morning propounding their advantages. Well, I'm afraid I don't like them at all. Once a month I'm responsible for selling tickets to a teenage disco here in Caloundra and we have approximately 900 kids, and 850 of them give me a plastic five dollar note. We have to get 900 kids into the disco in half an hour, and not only are they hard to handle at that pace but then I'm responsible for counting the money and preparing it for banking, and I hate the jolly things! You just can't imagine what a teenager can do to a plastic five dollar note.

I've got a good idea!

MARGARET: They are tearable, despite the people that are expounding their advantages. We get them through in all sorts of condition. If they've been through the washing machine there's very little printing left on them.

They seem to spring out. Doug Krepp was saying that he puts them in the drawer in his pub and he opens the drawer and they all fly out like a jack-in-the-box.

MARGARET: Well, Ian, I'll be honest with you: it's just as well no-one can get into my ticket office because I have them all over the floor—I walk on a carpet of fivers.

The letter from Mr Flint of Note Printing Australia made some good points. They're fully Australian made and they're much more durable and cost efficient, recyclable, environmentally friendly, good for the kiddies—no micro-organisms and all that sort of stuff.

MARGARET: Ian, I'd love that chap to come up here once a month and help me with the money in the ticket office, and I'm sure I'd shoot all his arguments down in flames! They're a curse. I don't like putting them into my ordinary cash purse because they keep bouncing out every time I open it. My money wants to get away from me fast enough!

Mr Flint does say that they're working on a new plastic, so you'll be able to fold them or something like that.

IAN TALKS WITH DOUG KREPP

Doug is licensee of a tavern up the top end of town in Kalgoorlie. He's got a little sign here: 'Give the feral fiver the flick. It's a Republican ploy'.

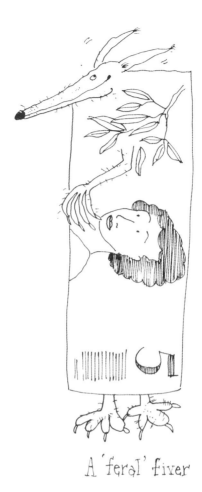

A 'feral' fiver

DOUG: Well, Macca, when you count the money in the morning the fivers keep jumping all over the place. They're the second worst thing in the world today, these fivers. You'd have to agree that the Pommie cricket side would have to be the worst thing in the world.

Oh, that's unfair; they're just going through a bad trot, mate.

DOUG: Anyway, the reason I said it's a Republican ploy is that when they printed these things they put poor old Bonzer Betty on them and everybody hates the notes so they're getting around to hating poor old Betty. Now, she's got nothing to do with the five dollar note. It escaped from Canberra about two years ago and I think if everyone in Australia, as complacent as we are, got together and started sending these things back tied to a housebrick and let the people in Canberra pick up the excess postage . . .

You don't mean the people in Canberra, they're nice people. You mean the politicians and the Mint, I suppose.

DOUG: Yes. They made these notes and sold the production overseas. I think if we put enough pressure on them we'd get rid of this useless five dollar note. Everyone that has to count money in business would know what I'm talking about. You have to have housebricks on your desk to count them because they keep jumping off the counter—they jump out of the till.

Because of the plastic they're springy. Yes, they're horrible, aren't they.

DOUG: I've taken a sample of the notes I've received in the last week and when they're bent they stay bent—they're like a crooked politician!

Oooh-ah! What a thing to say, Dougie! I said they were crook when they first came out but a lot of our coins are crook, too. We're never asked about these things. There's a lot of things we need to change in Australia, but listeners around Australia can help us give the feral fiver the flick.

DOUG: Yes. You attacked all those shopping trolleys years ago and you know how they behave now—you don't see them out on the streets. I'm going to start a movement here if everyone sends me enough fivers we'll get rid of them.

Oh, Doug!

DOUG: You don't think they'd fall for that one?

Well they say a fellow sold the Bridge again the other day!

The 31st of May 1992 marked the fiftieth anniversary of the submarine attack in Sydney Harbour—a Sunday, as it was fifty years ago, an exception being it was not full moon. That night was crystal clear, bright moonlight, cold and calm. May I outline some recollections of that night:

Aboard *Kuttabul* was a small group of Royal Navy sailors who had survived the action which resulted in the sinking of HMS *Prince of Wales* and HMS *Repulse*. Some of this group lost their lives on *Kuttabul*. Moored alongside, outboard of *Kuttabul*, was a Dutch submarine at the time the torpedo struck; apparently it was not seriously damaged and I am not aware that there were casualties aboard.

I relieved my opposite watchkeeper on the gun wharf steps just before midnight. He returned to *Kuttabul* and was one of those killed when the torpedo struck about ten to fifteen minutes after midnight.

Two torpedoes were fired at the USS *Chicago*; one carried on to explode below *Kuttabul*, the other struck a wooden pile of the gun wharf steps, burst its warhead, travelled up the bank alongside the wharf and came to rest completely out of the water. I spent the next twelve hours as its minder.

(There's a fifty-years-on talk with Alan Renouf at the end of this chapter.)

From: Horace Beazley, Mollymook, New South Wales

I just have to tell you what happened to Dad the other day. I can't let it go unknown! It was on Saturday morning. You see, we have a bit of trouble with the crows eating the eggs out of the chook pen on the other side of the dam, about 400 metres away from the back of the house. Dad got out of bed that morning, looked out the window, and there it was (a crow) sitting outside the pen, supposedly eating an egg. Being the pot shot he is he grabbed the rifle and crept to the back door. Praised himself that it didn't fly away when he opened the door.

Now comes the fluke part! He thought that as the chook pen was so far away, if he aimed about *two* feet above the crow's head and allowed for the bullet to drop: DEAD CROW! He fired, the crow jumped *three* feet in the air and dropped dead as a door nail. BUT, do you know what? It wasn't a crow, it was his best black rooster!! The bullet had gone through its wing and right into its heart. You guessed it, Christmas Dinner this year!!

The crows are still eating the eggs!!

From: Yvonne Brady, Curra, Queensland

Being a self-tutored trombonist I learned to play the instrument left-handed. I saw nothing wrong with this. I am naturally left-handed. My original trombone was cheap in both price and tone and I soon felt the need for something with a bit more 'oomph'. I was loaned a large bore 'B flat to F' bass trombone and I loved the sound of its deep, rich notes. However, in order to operate the valve trigger I needed a Heath Robinson system of bits of string. This did not help circulation in my right thumb!

I eventually saved enough coins to purchase a Yamaha large bore and the model I chose was reworked for left-handed operation——the rotary valve, plumbing and thumb-trigger repositioned accordingly. The changeover has not affected its tone or tuning.

It is quite amazing watching the facial expression of other trombonists when they pick the instrument up. I also receive strange looks from uninitiated conductors!

From: Kim Buckles, Mawson, Australian Capital Territory

Listening to your suggestion of a new verse for *Australia All Over* theme, you came up with the first line, viz:

There's a Radio Show that Australians all know

Of entrepreneurs, pollies and bankers . . .

but you said you couldn't find a word to rhyme with 'bankers', which I find very hard to believe, because the right word sprang into my mind immediately—— 'wankers'. Although I'm a little vague as to its meaning, it must be quite a respectable word as that was how I heard a very proper leading lady of the church from Rockhampton describe the people of Canberra to me. Interestingly the same word occurred to a nice little genteel nun with whom I work.

So your problem is solved, and I'm very happy to do some little thing for you in return.

PS   I'm very fortunate in that, while I'm a minister of the church, I have a job where I can listen to you right up till 9.50 am each Sunday and I don't have to hide a walkman under a cassock and surplice—I wouldn't miss your program for quids.

My father who is now in his eighties recalls when the first meeting of the businessmen and landowners occurred in Blackall in 1922 to rally financial support towards the establishment of the air service which we now know as Qantas.

My father was the son of a propery owner, Charles Millar, who at the time owned McFarlane Downs which was situated approximately twenty-eight miles from Blackall. My grandfather sent two of his eldest children, Aubrey and Vivienne, to the meeting. At the end of the meeting it was necessary to get back to the property and as there was only enough space on the plane for two people, the pilot, Hudson Fysh, flew Vivienne back to McFarlane Downs while Aubrey drove the co-pilot, Bird, back by car. Apparently Bird wasn't too happy about this as the roads were pretty rough. The plane landed on the airstrip at McFarlane Downs. Hudson Fysh and Bird stayed the night at the homestead and set off the next morning. The Millar family then contributed financially to the cause, although I don't know how much. Although Qantas hadn't really started Vivienne was actually the first female passenger. Something to be proud of!

I'm a shearers' cook. Shearers' cooks seem to have a reputation for being cranky old bastards. No one has ever bothered to ask us why. I am writing this to enlighten you all. Stoves, that's it—stoves. I mean, some of the places I go to the stoves have been there since 1885. They are starting to show some small signs of wear and tear. I use Mr Young Wood stoves mostly. Let me tell you about them. Some of you have to build a fire outside as well as inside to get warm, let alone hot; it will take a good two days for anything to cook. Then there are the ones where you have to wear fire-fighting equipment. You open the door which is dangerous because there are no sides in the oven. The flames see what you have in your hand and they eat it up, tray and all.

Then there are the ones that lean to one corner, mostly because over the last 150 years the foundations have shifted a metre or two. You put your casserole in the oven and the gravy runs out the dish down the back of your oven and comes out at your feet. All your cakes look like the Leaning Tower of Pisa. Now, we must not forget the ones that smoke. Every morning you go into the kitchen with a gas mask and coloured gloves so you can see through the smoke.

And people wonder why cooks are cranky old bastards!

I draw your attention to a couple of features of the Postcode List. What could be more symbolic of *Australia All Over* than that? It is a marvellous little document filled with musical and imaginative names, all reflecting the national character that created them.

Just by chance '3851 Kilmany' is immediately followed by '3764 Kilmore'. They must be a gruesome lot in Victoria. But the name that intrigues me comes from New South Wales—'2795 Dark Corner' doesn't show on any map I can find, but it sounds intriguingly dusky among the postcodes, and fills me with curiosity.

Others and I have noticed the beautiful way in which your older callers speak. Many of them would have had little or no formal education but it is a joy to listen to them as they recall their experiences. They speak with a respect for the English language and for their contemporaries. As one gentleman said a few weeks ago it was the way they were brought up. That says it all, doesn't it.

My reason for writing is that little monosyllable 'bloke' which is a favourite of yours by your admission. It's a very earthy kind of word, don't you think? There is something very basic, fundamental even, expressed by it. And there seems to be a measure of incorruptibility in the word; it's not open to the taint of popular usage or unwarranted journalese. Consider that other great word in the Aussie patois, 'mate', and see how it has suffered such unfortunate abasement once the political world got its hands on it. Looking after your mate takes on an entirely different meaning, totally opposed to the almost sacrificial sense of the Aussie mateship of yesteryear.

IAN TALKS WITH KATH THOMSON

At almost six o'clock one morning I said my usual 'Give us a ring on triple three twenty; you might be in Chillagoe (far North Queensland), just ring the operator and reverse the charges and say "I want to talk to Macca".' Next thing, Kath Thomson rings . . .

KATH: Hello Ian, it's Kath Thomson from Chillagoe. I took up the challenge.

How're you going, Kath? Tell everyone where Chillagoe is.

KATH: Well, Chillagoe's about three hours' drive west from Cairns, right in the bush. We own an eco lodge up here, but mostly we look after the mining people in the town.

What do they mine there?

KATH: There's Redgum Goldmine only about fifteen minutes away, and there are marble mines everywhere. They've been lying pretty dormant for a while but they're starting up again, so that's pretty good for the town. We've got drillers staying here at the moment and they're looking for special colours.

Kathy how long have you been there?

KATH: We've been here for fourteen years. When we first came we had the top pub, the Post Office Hotel. We were there for five years and then we built this camp.

What sort of land is it there?

KATH: It's green when it rains and it's very, very brown when it doesn't. It's full of lime bluffs and limestone caves, old mine sites, marble quarries, Aboriginal art and lots of fossil beds and gemstones.

What do they mine there?

KATH: It's a very big gold and copper mine.

It's a fairly isolated place, isn't it?

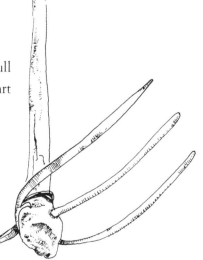

KATH: Yes, we haven't got a train any more. It came from Cairns to Chillagoe and then they stopped that and we're having a bit of a bun fight at the moment because the powers-that-be say we can have it, or Forsayth can have it, but we can't both have it back! So we had a deputation come through last week to see what we have to offer, then they've gone to Forsayth to see what they have to offer, then they'll make their recommendations.

Tell me about your day. What do you do there?

KATH: We get up at 4.30, make lots of lunches, cook cake and biscuits and get the men off to work.

And who else comes into Chillagoe?

KATH: Oh, we have lots and lots of tourists; they think it's unique staying here because it's very different.

And do you have prospectors coming through?

KATH: Yes, they're mostly looking for gold and copper.

And where were you from originally, Kath?

KATH: I was born in Ballina but I grew up in Sydney. My husband and I were married in Sydney and from Sydney we went to Papua New Guinea and from Papua New Guinea we came to Chillagoe.

Life's a big adventure, isn't it? You'd better give us a weather report.

KATH: It's fine, there's a gentle breeze and it's going to be a nice hot day.

Have you got to make sangers this morning?

KATH: I've done all the sandwiches and the cakes and I'm just waiting for the men to get up. They're a bit slow this morning.

Listen what sort of cake have you made? I just feel like a bit of cake . . .

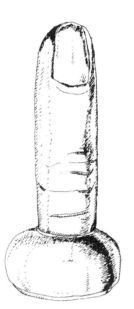

KATH: Well, I made jam drops this morning. You stick your finger in and then you put in the jam.

Isn't there a special implement? I don't think you're supposed to use your finger!

KATH: Oh, but this is the bush, Ian!

Fred and I were thrilled to bits with John Bourne's Jam Drop Hole Putter Inner. It works! It really does.

I am still amazed that a telephone call could give us, as well as the majority of the residents in Chillagoe, so much pleasure. Jim the postmaster has directed visitors to us and letters have found their way to the 'jam drop lady'.

Back to 'Perc', our JDHPI. I think John has a very marketable product. It should be there in the kitchen alongside the wooden spoon and the rolling pin.

From: Kath and Fred Thomson, Chillagoe, Queensland

Whilst walking down the road the other day I saw a herd of elephants in a paddock nearby.

I stopped and asked those elephants if they had ever heard of an elephant playing a mouth organ in a telephone booth. Those pachyderms became indignant, and argumentative. They told me that for an elephant to play a mouth organ in a telephone booth would be almost as impossible as for a human to play a trombone in a phone booth.

When I assured them that I had heard both on a radio program those pachyderms became so annoyed that they charged at me. Now I started running and a short way down the road I saw a telephone booth, and I remembered that if I rang *Australia All Over* I could have the charge reversed.

Ian, QUICKLY—I am still in the phone booth waiting for you to reverse the charge, or should I ring trunks and ask them?

From: Bob Nicol, Armidale, New South Wales

The way we are rubbishing Australia is quite frequently raised by listeners to your program.

Almost everywhere we drive, roadsides are deep in empty cans and chip packets, lolly wrappers, cartons and unidentifiable objects, flying and otherwise.

Appealing to the hip pocket seems the realistic answer. I think each State should employ thousands of inspectors, who, disguised as empty cartons, or abandoned shopping trolleys, lurk by roadsides, taking note of the numberplates of cars containing litterers and sending a fine through the mail. Perhaps the fine could be X number of feral $5 notes! Think of it. We'd solve the unemployment, rubbish and feral $5 problems in one fell swoop!

Australians all, let us purge the urge to litter the verge!

From: Judi Cox, Kenmore, Queensland

R ecently a recipe called for 'old potatoes', and I got to thinking—how long do you keep a potato before it is considered old, and was an OLD potato ever a NEW potato, or is he born old?

Now I've heard of baby chat potatoes, new potatoes and old potatoes, but what about the fellow in between—could he be a stud spud or a hip chip.

And it seems to be a bit irreverent to call a mature spud 'old'. Shouldn't he have a more distinguished title such as a later tater or a spry fry.

I thought I'd keep some new potatoes in the cupboard until they became old enough for my recipe, but all they did was slowly turn green and I ended up with a dud spud.

So hope you can help me, Ian—how old is an old potato and where and how does he spend his youth?

From: Pam Eyb, Cundletown, New South Wales

M y grandfather was an early bandmaster of the Horsham Town band and for years after his death my mother used to say, 'I wonder what happened to Dad's cornet—it was solid silver you know'.

I tried to assure her many times that a solid silver cornet would be very heavy— and worth a lot of money, but, to no avail; her answer to that was, 'I know it was heavy but Dad was a big man and Mother went mad at him when he imported it and said, "Fancy wasting all that money that we can ill afford".' (They were the local bakers in Horsham and had nine children.)

About twelve years ago (and with my mother still wondering every so often 'what happened to Dad's cornet—it was solid silver you know') at my bowls club I was practising with a chap who excused himself for an early departure as he had to go to band practice. Knowing that he had recently spent a few years in Horsham on business, I enquired whether he played in the band there.

He said he did all the time he was in Horsham, and I said, 'My grandfather was bandmaster there years ago', and he said, 'What was his name?' 'John Anderson', I replied. 'John Anderson's silver cornet', he exclaimed, and on asking what he knew about it he told the story.

'John Anderson's name is on the honour board and when we were shifting everything from the old, original weatherboard band hall to the new brick one the council built, we were cleaning everything out and tucked away under the stage on some stairs with old rubbish was this heavy old cornet in a case, and a music case with John Anderson's band arrangements for some great old marches etc. When we opened the cornet case we found a deed of gift from John Anderson donating his sterling silver cornet to the Horsham Town Band (now the Horsham City Band) in perpetuity.'

The unique cornet was, I believe, sent overseas to the makers for restoration and is now a prized possession of the Horsham City Band. My grandfather died in 1947 aged 84 and my mother in 1980 (also aged 84)—knowing what finally became of 'Dad's silver cornet'.

From: Alan Forster, Doncaster, Victoria

Two boys met, first day at school, looked at each other and immediately hated each other. They went to the same college and University, still not speaking. They both went into their professions. One went into the Navy, the other into the Church. Fifty years from their first meeting, they met face to face on London's Victoria Station. One was an Admiral in full dress, the other a Cardinal in red robes. The cardinal thought 'I should be the one to break the ice'. He went up to the Admiral and said 'Station Master, where does the train leave for Brighton?' The Admiral looked at the fat Cardinal and said 'Madam, in your condition, you shouldn't be travelling.'

From: Antonio Orsini, Cygnet, Tasmania

A group of friends were celebrating someone's birthday with a curry night at Toowoon Bay on the Central Coast. That's where I lived—in a prewar, fibro beach cottage less than a stone's throw from the surf.

I had made a great many chapatis. The recipe had said to roll them well—which I did . . . a bit too well. They came out when cooked like discs of baked clay! Having rather a lot left over, as only a few were used as drink coasters, the next best thing was to use them as a frisby. We retired to the balcony overlooking the Pacific Ocean and sailed them off into the black beyond the breakers. They flew extremely well—simple things amuse simple minds, especially after several hearty curries and a few refreshing ales. It was a happy party.

My friend Mark then quipped, 'It's chapati and I'll fly if I want to'!

You will no doubt remember the song of the 1950s or 1960s—'It's my party and I'll cry if I want to'. There was a brief silence as our curry and ale-affected brains got into gear and then uproar rose over the night. It was one of the most memorable off-the-cuff quips.

From: Ian Oelrichs, Ballina, New South Wales

The drover is not dead! A bit thin on the ground maybe, but the working drover still exists. My wife and I have just come back from Alexandria Station in the Northern Territory where I was a jackeroo forty years ago. Last year they sent six mobs on foot from Sandan Outstation to the Channel Country, five or six weeks away.

Alexandria has to be one of the greatest places on Earth. Over 6000 square miles (once 11,200 square miles) of magnificent rolling downs, 60,000 head of fine cattle, organised with an efficiency our bureaucrats should take a look at. There are vast changes since I was there working, but the spirit of the place remains. We were received very generously and although most of the people I knew are now dead, at least someone knew them and knew what had happened to them. I met the sons of a couple. I was also able to trace my old boss, Ken McGuire, and telephoned him when I got home. He has always been a bit of a hero of mine. I never saw him back away from trouble, whether a bad ringer, a bad beast or a bad horse.

Take heart; the old bush lives on!

From: Barry Laver, Bowen, Queensland

I have been told by two old bakers that the reason modern city bakeries do not make good bread is that their flour is too fresh. It is basically wheat one morning and bread the next, when the best bread is made with aged flour. That is why country bakers and suburban hot bread shops, who use bagged flour, make better bread. Also the reason city bread has a texture of foam plastic is that they produce the yeast by a fermentation process and a wet slurry is used that results in a very even distribution of the yeast in the dough; when compressed yeast is used the yeast is not so evenly spread and the resulting bread has the non-uniform texture.

From: David Canaway, Avondale Heights, Victoria

GILES AND OUR LAND

During his exploration of Australia's interior in the 1870s, Ernest Giles, who died of pneumonia in 1897 aged 52 and was buried in Coolgardie, would have experienced all the hazards, beauty and vastness of this unique continent.

BALGO HILLS MISSION

Eleanor Watson, who teaches in a remote community, the Balgo Hills Mission in the Kimberleys where people still speak their own language, sent these photographs showing some of their activities. The Easter celebrations, a mixture of ritual Catholicism and Aboriginality, went on for five days! Digging for bush onions; Eleanor with Earnie Bridge, her Aboriginal friend for thirty-five years and the local MP.

fter reading this clipping from a 1971 newspaper I wondered 'where did we go wrong?'

HAPPY DAY

Recently, I travelled on a train with a little old man. He had travelled far and seen much. I asked him if he could recall his happiest day. He smiled: 'This is one I always remember. It was a summer day with hot sun and warm breeze. In the morning, I weeded the garden, then cleaned my boots. I washed the windows and ran some errands for my mother. When that was done, I went across a paddock to the river, and there, under the shade of a gum tree, I lay and read *Treasure Island*. I ate an orange and a pennyworth of mints.

From: Dora

Here's another example of how too often we Australians kowtow to the Americans, and are in danger of losing all the interesting corners of our culture in favour of the American culture.

Here in Perth (and maybe elsewhere in Western Australia) there is a loud TV advertising campaign pushing big hamburgers, but their way of stressing how big the burgers are is to say, 'Burgers the size of Texas'. This is in Western Australia, the biggest state in Australia; Western Australia, a state so big it makes Texas look like Tasmania; Western Australia, the state as big as half of all the USA. How come people living in Western Australia can (without thinking) accept advertising claiming that Texas is big?

Western Australia—THAT's big.

From: David O'Connor, Wilson, Western Australia

I heard the old canecutter bloke who was excellent. He was right; canecutting was very laborious work and especially, as he said, because it was piece work, like shearing, there was always a kind of edge to it, with blokes pushing one another along. It's better known in shearing, because there was usually a race to see who would ring a shed, but canecutting wasn't the same in that the gangs were smaller and so not so many blokes were pitted against each other as in the big sheds at shearing time. Usually, too, because all cheques were shared equally, blokes in a cutting gang usually were about the same standard and speed; if you couldn't keep your tally up to the other blokes they'd soon let you know that you had better go and find a place in a gang that was more your speed. And of course, the ganger and the faster cutters would push you along to try to keep up with them. The more tons, the more dollars, and you were expected to pull your weight.

When I made the two 'Back to Innisfail' programs a few years ago with Keith Richards, I talked to a few of the old cutters in the Innisfail area, and really most of the blokes said that they didn't mind the mechanical harvesters coming in; which is the way I felt about it. As one old-timer put it, 'Men shouldn't have to work like that, always keeping an eye on the other blokes in the gang and trying to push harder all the time to keep up'.

The good things about the old cane seasons were, of course, the stir of life they brought to the little towns where the mills were. From December through to March would be the Wet, of course, with nothing much going on save planting, ploughing out etc. Then April, May, June was all growing time. Most mills geared up to start late June/early July, midwinter in the North, and the little towns that had been sleepy hollows for six months braced themselves for the harvest. There was always a big influx of men just at the beginning of the season, cutters and blokes who worked the seasons in the mills; and a town could often nearly double the population in a fortnight as these fellows all arrived—by train, pushbike or even on foot in some cases. This flood of new faces brought the townships to life, of course, and there was always a stir of excitement, of anticipation, and of commerce at the beginning of the season.

From: Bill Scott, Warwick, Queensland

About the imminent closure of the Meekatharra RFDS. I was not aware of it although I knew it was only a matter of time. The Wyndham base was closed a few years ago and Darwin VJY has gone over to the St John's Ambulance people. While modern communications promise that everything will be better, faster and cheaper, it means more and more concentration into populated areas and technology only the well-heeled can afford. Ironically, the people who need communication most, such as the stranded traveller and the sick station kid, are more and more disadvantaged. What would 'Flynn of the Inland' say? Another bit of quintessential Australia is being dismantled to make way for commercially-driven approaches to living and . . . dying.

In 1963 I was able to save two children from a terrible death through lack of water. Help for the children was obtained through the RFDS. The mother, who had perished, had to be buried. Eight months later, on Boxing Day, I nearly perished when my car burnt out in the Gibson Desert and I was found after three long days. On that occasion the message I had left for the RFDS had not been passed on. If it had been, I would have been saved much misery.

While more and more vehicles have HF sets, it is obvious that many people simply will go without as the cost of the new technology will be prohibitive. Centralisation means less local know-how, less commitment, greater formality and the big brother approach to matters which need an understanding and a delicate hand. In the end, the bottom line is that rare and crucial expertise has to make way for book-oriented technical expertise you can pick up at your local college, combined with public-service-style working habits. Put differently, it means quality will be exchanged for elusive savings that never reach the community and relevance and reliability will be traded for distant and impersonal bureaucratic control.

From: Mark de Graaf, Casuarina, Northern Territory

How about the Sydney Rugby League Grand Final!! They use imported footballs and then provide the ultimate insult by IMPORTING someone to demonstrate the art of screaming to 'gee up' the crowd. If they do feel it necessary to wake the crowd up before the big game, the least the authorities could do is to ensure that Australian entertainers are utilised.

From: Col White, Innisfail, Queensland

It would be more than fifty years ago that I was handed a short story which I've kept all these years.

A COUNTRY WC

A young couple, soon to be married, had been looking at houses in the country. Having satisfied themselves that one certain house would be suitable they made their way home. On the way the young man noticed the girl's thoughtful look so asked the reason why.

'Edward, did you notice where the WC was?' But he could not remember having seen it. So they decided to write the owner to ask where it was located.

The owner was an elderly gentleman who was puzzled as to the meaning of 'WC'. He finally came to the conclusion that they must be asking about the Wesleyan Church. So he replied as follows . . .

Dear Sir,
I am pleased to inform you that the WC is situated about nine miles from the

house. It is capable of seating about 250 persons. I suppose that nine miles is a long way if you are in a habit of going regularly, and that is unfortunate. However, I am sure you will be glad to know that a great number of people take their lunch with them and make a day of it. And there are some people who always seem to be running late, they come by car and arrive just in time.

It will be interesting for you to know that our daughter was married in the WC. In fact, it was there that she met her husband when they happened to sit together one day. Oh, how I remember that wedding on account of the real rush for seats. There must have been ten people on a seat normally holding only two. It was so wonderful to catch the expressions on their faces. My brother was there that day too. In fact he has gone to the WC regularly ever since he was christened there. Just recently a wealthy man who goes regularly to the WC had a bell erected over it to be rung every time a member enters.

A bazaar is to be held next door, and the proceeds are to provide plush seats, as members feel this has been a long-felt need. My wife and I are getting old now, and we do not go as regularly as we used to go. It is six years since we last went, and I can assure you it pains us greatly not to be able to go more regularly. Yours Faithfully,

From: **Lester Hawkes, Redland Bay, Queensland**

Ian Talks with Alan Renouf

Tell me, what were you doing fifty years ago?

ALAN: I was the Acting Adjutant of the 17th Infantry Battalion, which was one of the three battalions charged with the defence of the northern beaches from Manly to Palm Beach. One can wonder now what use that would have been had the Japanese come in, but that's by the way! On that particular night I was awakened by a signal that said the batallion must move immediately to its pre-prepared positions on the beaches, so I woke up the CO and about 6.30 in the morning the battalion got on its way and after a little while the CO said, 'Have you got any idea what all this is about'. I said, 'No, sir, there was nothing in the signal, just the order to move to the beaches'. I had what in those days was called a portable radio—although it was so bloody heavy it was barely portable—so I said, 'I'll tune into the ABC News and see what they say'. He said, 'Don't be so silly, that'd be a military secret', but I thought it was worth trying and sure enough it came through on the ABC news that the Japanese submarines were in Sydney Harbour. So that was how one of the battalions charged with the defence of Sydney came to find out the news! I suppose the bangs alerted newsmen to find out what was going on.

We can't realise now what it was like, but it would have been chaos, really, if Sydney had been attacked. Australia was not prepared for war at all.

ALAN: No, I don't think anybody in Sydney thought this could happen, and obviously that was one of the purposes of the Japanese raid. Mind you, I think it's true to say that before that there was an incident where a Japanese submarine shelled Sydney. I can remember that very well, too, because I was on leave that weekend and I was coming home from a dance at the Bronte Surf Club on the Sunday night and suddenly I heard artillery shells going overhead. Being rather stupid, I suppose, I thought it was a funny time of the day for the North Head batteries to be practising! But it was a submarine landing a few shells in Sydney, just to say, 'We're here, mate, watch out!'.

How long did you stay in charge of the Northern Beaches defences?

ALAN: Oh, shortly after that I was taken into the AIF. I'd volunteered but recruitment had been held up and I was on the waiting list.

That wasn't many men, was it, to protect such an area?

ALAN: Well, I took this up with the CO one day. I had a platoon of twenty men and one Bren gun to defend Harbord beach. The CO used to come down to inspect us from time to time, and one day I said, 'Sir, I don't understand the strategy behind this. What do we do if the Japanese come in?' He said, 'You stay and die'. I said, 'Well, that wouldn't serve any purpose. What could twenty men do against what would probably be thousands landing on the beach'. He said, 'Ours not to reason why, ours but to do and die!'. But I would have thought the better military strategy—and it's easy to say this in retrospect—would have been to concentrate such forces as we had in a place like French's Forest and when a landing was made in a particular place to send the whole force there to try to repulse it.

Alan Renouf was an ambassador and a head of foreign affairs. Interestingly, your first posting as an ambassador was to Yugoslavia—is that right, Alan?

ALAN: Not my first posting as an ambassador, but I was the first ambassador sent to Yugoslavia when we established diplomatic relations in about 1966. Tito was there and I got to know him quite well. He was an interesting character; he had a wonderful sense of humour. Of course, some Yugoslavs would call him a butcher from the war years, but when I knew him he was quite a benevolent dictator: he never shot anybody or put them up against a wall or tortured them, he just put them under house arrest if they fell into disfavour. But he once made a remark to me which sticks in my mind, particularly since the fighting broke out in Yugoslavia, and that was, 'You know, Mr Ambassador, I'm the only Yugoslav in Yugoslavia. As you must know, when everybody else is asked what nationality they are they say a Croat, or a Serb, or a Montenegran, or a Macedonian, etc. I always say I'm a Yugoslav, but I know full well I'm the only Yugoslav that says that. You know, this is a very divided country and I've held it together, but when I go God knows what will happen'. His words were very prophetic, as it turned out!

They say that every man has a lurking wish
to be thought considerable in his own place

'OPPY' OPPERMAN

MOTHERS AND MOTHER'S DAY

'Mother's Day' as Lorna (my mum) says, is every day of the year. If you can't be nice to your mum every day, but need a special day, then there's something wrong. We've never run a special Mother's Day program, but everyone's got a mother and we've collected these letters and poems together as a tribute to the people who make the world go round.

A couple of people have said to me right out of the blue——you know, pushed their way through a crowd, confronted me and said, 'You must have a lovely mother' and then just disappeared. Quite unnerving really.

Well, she is, and as well as that she's been a great help and guide for the program. She found 'I Made a 100 In The Backyard At Mum's' and told me about it, and it was at her request that I played more and more Australian music back in 1982. She's a good judge of a poem and a great comfort to all around her.

JUST FOR MUMS!!!!

(With thanks to Banjo Patterson!)

There was movement in the classroom
as the word it got around,
'Hey kids, it's almost Mother's day!'

The kids they got together to work out
what to buy
For they wished to make this Sunday
just like cream and apple pie.

They thought of books and flowers and music
It was all so hard to choose it
And some of them had only got a few
dollars to pay.

But as they sat and thought
They realised the present need not
be bought
For what would make the nicest gift of all?
A HUG!!!!

From: **Eloise Smart, aged 10, Mosman, New South Wales**

A Mother's Day poem written by Mr A J McIntyre of Hervey Bay.

CALL ME MUM

I can change a smelly nappy, without bringing up my meal,
I can bathe a squirming infant, No matter how it squeals,
I can wipe off runny noses, Clean up puddles as they come,
I'm a female jack-of-all trades, But the kids they call me Mum.

I can patch up cuts and bruises, break up a teenies' fight,
I can soothe a baby's fears, in dark hours of the night,
I can mix an infant's bottle, just by rule of thumb,
I'm a Doctor, Nurse, and counsellor, round here I'm known as Mum.

I can mend a pair of trousers, or a dress that's kinda torn,
I can feed the healthy appetites that start at early morn,
My daughter tells me secrets, my son thinks I'm his chum,
To my husband, I'm the Missus, but the name I like is Mum.

So I pause this day each year, this special time in May,
And quietly count my blessings, and this I have to say,
My life gets pretty hectic, doing one thing, then another.
All the year I'm known as Mum, today my title's—MOTHER.

From: **Mrs Shirley Ling, Devonport, Tasmania**

Because Mother's Day is near I am writing to pass on some information that ties in with your extract on the life and times of the great Australian basso—Malcolm McEachern.

During World War I my late mother, Ina Davidson, toured with Malcolm giving concerts down Australia's eastern seaboard. She had a beautiful operatic soprano voice and Malcolm and a touring English entrepreneur, Humphrey Bishop, wanted to send her to Italy to further her studies. Lack of finance and the war prevented this, but she cycled thirty miles to Launceston each weekend for singing lessons.

She married soon after the war and for thirty years shared her many musical talents as a singer, pianist and church organist, giving free tuition to any keen and talented person. It is a great joy to see these gifts coming out in my grandchildren.

From: **Ada Robinson, Devonport, Tasmania**

You were talking about rugby and knitting yesterday and the proximity of Mother's Day put me in mind of one of my father-in-law's recollections.

In the late 'twenties he was courting my wife's mother, who was a designer and pattern knitter for Paton & Baldwin. He played Rugby Union for St George and New South Wales and his fiancee attended the matches with her knitting, rugby not being her favourite pastime. One day he suffered a crunching tackle just before half time and was taken to hospital by ambulance, with all the accompanying noise, to check for broken bones and concussion. He had no lasting injuries and was returned to the ground at full time still in rugby gear. His fiancee's comment was, 'Did you have a good game? I didn't see much of you in the second half'!

From: **Peter Cannell, Heathmont, Victoria**

Dear Macca,

We are sending you a Mother's Day Recipe to share with your listeners. It will tell them what ingridens they will need to make Mother's Day fantastic. It all so tell's them the metherd in case they don't know what to do.

You can give the recipe to your mum on Mother's Day if you like. We hope you enjoy it. We relly like your program.

We hope all your *listeners* that are mum's enjoy it, and have a brilyent Mother's Day. God bless you!

2F 1992 and Miss Flanagan.

PS. I hope you can understand the spelling! Jo Flanagan

Recipe for a fantastic Mothers Day

Ingredients

1 delicious breakfast in bed
99 armfuls of hugs
87 kisses (sloppy ones if you like)
100 heartfuls of love
5-10 medium cups of tea (or coffee)
1 gift given with a kiss
1 surprise barbecue lunch
1000 rays of sunshine
840 giggles of laughter
12 hours of smiles
A family (any size will do)
1 beautiful mum

Method :

Mix the kisses, hugs, love, sunshine, laughter and smiles into the family, stirring quickly. Shake over the mum for the whole day. At just the right time present the breakfast, cups of tea, lunch and gift.

WARNING
At no time is the mum allowed to touch any electric appliances of she is likely to short circuit.

NANNA'S BISCUIT TIN

No sticky fingers ever lived until they grappled in
the delightful hidden treasures of Nanna's biscuit tin.
Containing healing powers denied to science for years,
that flooded out to heal skun knees and dry up sobs and tears.

When it diiiidn hit the wicket and I waaaasn realy out
Nanna understood, she knew what life was all about.
Going to the cupboard and reaching to the back
She withdrew the medication to destroy a blues attack.

As the tears and crumbs combined with a little dose of 'never mind',
The biscuit tin would work its charm and leave the daily woes behind.
It mattered not how many kids were sorry sick or sore,
We never saw the bottom there was always plenty more.

When the baby yelled and screamed with new teeth pushing through,
an Anzac munched upon the mat would fix that problem too.
Melting moments, kisses, and rock cakes by the score,
dispensed with jokes and laughter, and ice cold drinks galore.

And so it was through youthful years when study times got tough,
A quick stop off at Nanna's and that tin would do its stuff.
The smell of Nanna's cooking would greet us at the gate,
and it somehow didn't matter if assignments went in late.

Angels come in aprons with glasses and grey hair,
teaching kids to laugh at troubles, to reach out, love and care.
Instilling priceless character to build a life upon,
It's easier to walk the path where Nanna's light has shone.

Let the secret powers of Nanna's love colour every child,
Let each kid lick the mixing spoon approved with Nanna's smile.
For Nannas know the way to peace so let us raise our banners
and start a conservation push for biscuit tins and Nannas.

From: Geoff Miller, Devonport, Tasmania

This poem was given to me by a loving daughter. You know, mothers really are the most taken-for-granted beings. They care for everyone and they're always there, so take time on this one day of the year to show you care, because one day they won't be there.

MOTHER MAKING

When the Good Lord was creating
mothers, he was into his sixth day of over
time when an angel appeared.

'You're doing a lot of fiddling around on
this one, Lord,' the angel said.

And the Lord said: 'Have you read
the specifications on this order?

She has to be completely washable
but not plastic, have 180 movable parts,
all replaceable, run on black tea and
left-overs, have a lap which
disappears when she stands up, and
a kiss that can cure anything from
a broken leg to a broken heart, and
six pairs of hands.'

The angel shook her head slowly
and said: 'Six pairs of hands. No way'.

'It's not the hands which are
causing me the trouble,' the Lord said.

'It's the three pairs of eyes
that mothers have to have. One pair
sees through closed doors when she asks
'What are you kids doing in there?'
when she already knows.

Another in the back of her head
so she can see what she shouldn't
but needs to know.

And of course, the ones in the front that
can look at a child when he gets himself in
trouble and say 'I understand and I love you'
without uttering so much as a word.'

'I can't rest,' said the Lord. 'I'm so close now.'

'Already I have one who heals herself when she's sick, can feed a family of six on half a kilogram of mince and can get a nine-year-old to stand under the shower.'

The angel circled the model of a mother very slowly.

'It's too soft,' the angel cried,' But tough,' the Lord said excitedly.

'Can it think?'

'Not only can it think, but it can reason and compromise,' said the Lord.

Finally the angel bent over and ran a finger across the cheek.

'There's a leak,' she pronounced.

'It's not a leak,' the Lord said, 'It's a tear.'

'What's it for?'

'It's for joy, sadness, disappointment, pain, loneliness and pride.'

'You're a genius,' the angel said.

The Lord looked sombre and said:
'I didn't put it there.'

From: **Mary de Courcey, Rangewood**

I was a bit taken aback by the comment concerning Mum having to bat last or not at all after fielding all day. It reminded me of an incident here.

I have three sons (10, 8 and 6) who are avid fans of Rugby League and as you can imagine there is a constant three-man team careering up and down the yard with a football.

The other day my son William, being the youngest and the odd man out, complained in tears that no-one wanted to be on his team. I said, 'Wait until I've finished washing-up and I'll be on your team'. He went off happily and smugly announced that Mum was going to be on his team. I heard gales of laughter and saw the other two rolling about, laughing. It wasn't so funny when I realised they were laughing at me. I decided THIS WAS WAR, left the washing-up and proceeded to take up the challenge.

Well, I even surprised myself. Not noted for my sporting prowess, I got the ball and ran and ran and stiff-armed, weaved, etc. That night my status was somewhat enhanced when my eldest reported, 'You know what, Dad—Mum made three tries!'

The playing field has been levelled at our place now and when Mum appears in the yard the cry goes up, 'Will you be on our team, Mum?'

I hope the Mums who previously had to field all day will now go out and bat for themselves—they might surprise themselves—and others.

From: Barbara Campbell, Condamine, Queensland

I'm sending you a beautiful poem my mum wrote one day while she was watching her long-awaited home being built.

It's strange how your home town always seems to call you back, no matter how many years later. In the 1950s my great-great-grandfather, Alexander Waddell, was the first to discover gold in the Araluen Valley, near where my parents now have their home. With very little money and six children our family moved around to wherever Dad had work and I don't know how Mum was always able to have food on the table and how we always had nice clothes and new shoes when we needed them. Christmas must have been a nightmare for them—what must they have missed out on themselves so we could have all those things?

It's wonderful now to see Mum and Dad settled in their new home after waiting for it for half a century. Thanks, Mum and Dad, for always being there.

PS: If Mum's poem is read out she probably won't speak to me again, but I'll take that chance!

IT WOULD BE NICE

It would be nice
To read at night
By a light that is good for your eyes
To sit by the fire
Or lie in bed
And read to your heart's desire

It would be nice
To turn a hot tap
And wash all the dirty dishes
To rinse out the cloth
And wipe the sink down
Life is so full of wishes.

It would be nice
To have a hot bath
At the time that suited me most
Not when the pump's running
Or when the drum is just boiling
And then I will spoil the roast.

It would be nice
To do all the washing
In water that's warm for my hands
Not drive down to Frank's
Then haul it all back
And find that my thumbs just won't work.

It would be nice
To make cakes by the dozen
In a stove in an ordin'ry oven
Not gather the wattle
And get the fire right
For a fling in the old campoven.

It would be nice
To turn on a tap
And water the garden with ease
Not draw off the petrol
Then start up the pump
And find the black pipe has been squeezed.

It would be nice
To always feel clean
Instead of all grotty and rough
To always wear clothes
That smell of a rose
Instead of pollard and kittens and smoke.

But it is nice
To see our house
Grow like a tree
Above all the land that is ours

SOME CHARACTERS

Some of the 'characters' who have appeared on the program: Alex Pike who mined for gold around Kalgoorlie for many years. As a result of our talk he made contact with the family of miners he'd met back in the 1920s; the lovely Gilbert, now over ninety, a great favourite of listeners; Doug Krepp the Kalgoorlie licensee sums up what very many Australians think about 'feral fivers'; Vince Clancy the former cane cutter keeps me company on his harmonica. Incidentally, that great Australian Test batsman, Peter Burge, stands right behind Vince wearing a turquoise shirt. They used to play in whites in his day! And talking of 'greats', world champion Lionel Rose strums a tune with the Howie Brothers.

'FAVOURITE THINGS'

We like the "G'Day, G'Day" Song.

Lambs and kids…The Hallett children, Jack, Becky and Katie, are all smiles. The girls sent a book of their pictures, including the G'day song.

· · · · · · · · · · · ·

The children from 3R Alice Springs attempt the SAO song. They sent jokes too.

The lightening flashed, the thunder roared.
The dogs ran under the houses
The magpie sat on his windy perch
And the wind blew up his trousers.
Ms Rumball taught us becaus we
like magpies on Australia
All Over.
Amanda

And soon I can make it a home for us all
By the river we do love the most
Where the kids can all come
And bring their kids home too
To Granny and Pop to make toast.

From: Helen Waddell, Eden, New South Wales

PHONE CALLS FROM OVERSEAS

Lt Col. Steve Ayling, Cambodia Peace Keeping Force 7 June 1992

Keith Parker, Japan 19 July 1992

Tracey, Davis Base Station, Antarctica 20 September 1992

David Crisp, Texas, USA 8 November 1992

Sister Jean, Papua New Guinea 7 February 1993

Major David Tyler, Somalia 21 February 1993

Peter Abbott, Mt Seymour, Canada 14 March 1993

Graham Morrison, Casey Base Station, Antarctica 25 April 1993

Derek Mills, Port Moresby, Papua New Guinea 25 April 1993

Major Melva Crouch, Cambodian Anzac Service 25 April 1993

Allan Humphries, Hong Kong 2 May 1993

Steve Tancred, Memphis, Tennessee, USA 23 May 1993

Graeme Armstrong, Casey Base Station, Antarctica, Mid-winter Dinner 30 May 1993

Tim Fisher MP, Khyber Pass 11 July 1993

David Calphy, Idaho, USA 8 August 1993

Boyd Johnson, Driffield, Yorkshire, UK 12 September 1993

Mick Slocum, Bangkok, Thailand, 19 September 1993

Allan Sullivan, Fukuoka, Japan 17 October 1993

Allan Sullivan, Nagano, Japan 24 October 1993

Mary McDougall, Port Moresby, Papua New Guinea 24 October 1993

Martin Corben, Loch Ness, Scotland 31 October 1993

Graeme Armstrong, Casey Base Station, Antarctica, coming home after twelve months
    5 December 1993

Lance Corporal Anthony Simmons, Signaller Glen Noonan, Kelly Irvine, Western
    Sahara 19 December 1993

Paul Chambers, on freeway between Louisana and Texas, USA 6 February 1994

Simon, Botswana 6 March 1994

John Phillips, Kokoda Hotel, Papua New Guinea 13 March 1994

Bill Fordyce, London RAF Base, Great Escape reunion 27 March 1994

Bill Chubb, Kutubu, Papua New Guinea Oil Project 10 April 1994

David Hill, Jakarta, Indonesia 10 April 1994

Nigel Russell, Gobi Desert, Mongolia 17 April 1994

Father Brian, London, UK 15 May 1994

Ross Dominey, Napier, New Zealand 22 May 1994

Michael Thatchell, Bangkok, Thailand 5 June 1994

David Graham, Grong, Norway 12 June 1994

Dr Peter Burns, Rhinelander, Wisconsin USA 19 June 1994

Keefer Darcy, Port Moresby Papua New Guinea 26 June 1994

Rosie Butteridge, Suva, Fiji 10 July 1994

Kirsten, Kumamoto Japan 10 July 1994

Olivia, Officer cadet, Australian Defence Force Academy, in Singapore where she won a course award 10 July 1994

Paul McCann, Bath, UK, Emus School Boys' Cricket 17 July 1994

ISLANDS

Peena Geia, Palm Island 22 November 1992

Dave, Norfolk Island 7 February 1993

Sandra Earle, Thursday Island 14 February 1993

Dr Peggy Rismuller, Kangaroo Island, researching echidnas 11 April 1994

Rowan Foley, Fraser Island 13 June 1994

Julianne, Phillip Island 27 June 1993

Scottie, Ross Island, Antarctica 5 September 1993

Shirley, Bribie Island 19 December 1993

Jean, Flinders Island 20 February 1994

Jan Herman, Umbakumba, Groote Eylandt 27 February 1994

Greg Geeves, Gunoona, Mornington Island 3 April 1994

Alex Pinkster, Thevenard Island, 150 km off Onslow WA 29 May 1994

Barry Platts, Mornington Island 12 June 1994

SHIPS, BOATS

Geoff Walpole, HMAS *Perth*, off Magnetic Island 10 May 1992

Sue Kennett, USS *Blue Ridge*, Cleveland Bay, 15 miles off Townsville 10 May 1992

Nigel Scullion, *Killidris*, near Arnhem Bay 24 May 1992

Penny Von Oosterzee, on a sailing ship between Darwin and Cairns, looking for turtles 19 July 1992

Ann Barker, Yacht *Wairangi*, off Bathurst Island, the Ambon races, 56 boats off to Indonesia 26 July 1992

David Jeffries, Yacht *Jupiter*, Cook's voyage 30 August 1992

Captain John Lord, HMAS *Hobart*, Coral Sea, returning home 23 August 1992

Wade Hughes, HMAS *Warrnambool*, Victoria, Admezca Surfboat Race 8 November 1992

Commander Frank Allica, *Young Endeavour*, south of Fiji 29 November 1992

Dennis, *Escape*, on the Barrier Reef 6 December 1992

Denis, outside Dongara W A, crayfish season 20 December 1992

Russell, Barrier Reef, building a floating pontoon 20 December 1992

Richard, skipper, Steel Challenge Race, on their way to Capetown 14 February 1993

Don Macintyre, Yacht *Buttercup*, coming home from Antarctica 14 February 1993

John, Yacht *Villella*, off Curtis Island Qld 3 April 1994

Commander Graham Johnston, Coral Sea, in the middle of Cyclone Roger 14 March 1993

Ian Smith, captain *Sea Cat*, Tasmania 14 March 1993

Nigel Scullion, *Kallidris*, in Napier Broome Bay 28 March 1993

Mike, *El Torico*, in Torres Strait, blind kayakers 28 March 1993

Bill, Yacht *Le Truck*, 450 miles north of Exmouth WA 23 May 1993

Mike Steel, off coast of Wyndham, WA 11 July 1993

Wade Hughes, HMAS *Warrnambool*, off Portland Vic. 17 October 1993

Captain Slim Hughes, *Iron Whyalla*, coast of NSW, heading for Turkey 30 January 1994

Captain Slim Hughes, *Iron Whyalla*, south of Italy 13 March 1994

Nigel Scullion, *Kallidris*, The Kimberley 13 March 1994

Captain Slim Hughes, *Iron Whyalla* 1500 miles east of the Cape of Good Hope, off Madagascar 17 April 1994

Nigel Scullion, *Kallidris*, bottom of the Gulf of Carpentaria, off 'Bing Bong' Station 24 April 1994

Darren, on a prawn trawler, Gulf of Carpentaria 15 May 1994

Captain Slim Hughes, *Iron Whyalla*, Makassar Strait off the east coast of Borneo 22 May 1994

Michael Marley, ship's officer, HMAS *Hobart*, Pearl Harbour, Hawaii 29 May 1994

Captain Slim Hughes, *Iron Whyalla*, anchored off Port Kembla 12 June 1994

Captain Tom Harris, *Iron Pacific* (Australia's largest ship) at Garden Island, Sydney 19 June 1994
Nigel Scullion, *Kallidris*, off Port Essington 19 June 1994
Gary, crayfishing boat off Dongara WA 26 June 1994
Annette, fishing boat, Murray River Vic 26 June 1994

PLANES

Captain Warwick Tainton, flying over Gulf of Carpentaria 1 November 1992
Gavin Gilchrist, science reporter, in helicopter over the Blue Mountains 2 May 1993
Ian McFee, in air, motor glider, Australian Championships 29 November 1993
Ian Button, Coast Watch plane over Ulladulla, Blessing of the Fleet 3 April 1994

TRAINS

Gary, Train 3801, Brisbane to Casino 14 November 1993
Graham, Southern Aurora, outskirts of Melbourne 21 November 1993

MISCELLANEOUS

David Hewitt, Jupiter Well (most remote telephone box) 5 July 1992
Geoff Hocking, Kalimantan Coal Mine, Borneo 10 April 1994

It always rains at the end of a drought

PEOPLE AND PLACES

One of the wonderful aspects of the program are the gems of Australian history, about its people and places, that are revealed by letters, interviews and phone calls. Rosemary Thompson, the daughter of the late and great Australian naturalist David Fleay, wrote in 1989:

My father established his own fauna reserve in the middle of the Gold Coast without any help in 1952 and opened it to the public seven days a week. He worked hard to make ends meet to maintain not only his fauna collection but also the daily influx of sick and injured birds and animals. He received no government aid and was perhaps an original 'greenie' when he co-founded the Wildlife Preservation Society of Queensland twenty-five years ago.

Whenever you play 'Ringo the Dingo' it reminds me of the Beatles' visit to Brisbane in 1964 when they requested father to send a koala and a dingo pup to their hotel room. They were delighted and promptly christened the pup 'Ringo'. This led to a wonderful newspaper cartoon of Ringo Star feeding his namesake with a chicken 'drumstick'. It was amusing to hear a caller say that when he visited my parents in 1932 with the Toorak Central class my father seemed more enthused by a marsupial birth than that of my sister, Betty. It reminded me that nearly thirty years ago when my son Phillip was born (father's first grandson) his Taipan snake 'Alexandra' stole most of my thunder by laying her first clutch of eggs the same day.

Father photographed the last Tasmanian Tiger in captivity in Hobart Zoo in 1933, receiving a playful nip on his rump from the animal in the process. His attempt to secure a pair of Tasmanian Tigers for breeding purposes was frustrated by red tape. When he finally managed to take an expedition to Tasmania in search of the 'Tiger' in 1947 it was unfortunately too late.

He handed over the sixty-five acre reserve to the people of Australia in 1983, a pristine green belt in the midst of the Gold Coast concrete.

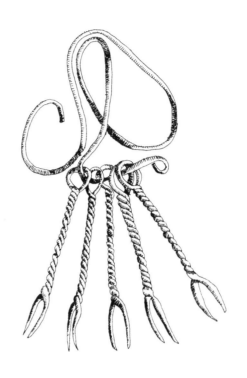

You recently broadcast from the Old Andado homestead which used to be my home in the late 'forties and early 'fifties.

My father and mother, Charlie and Jess Paige, managed the place for Alf Turner who is affectionately known throughout Central Australia as 'The Old Border'. When Alf sold Andado we moved to Bushy Park Station just sixty miles from the Alice. At that time Molly and Mac Clark were on the neighbouring property, Alcoota.

At the time we lived at Andado we had no modern conveniences whatsoever. Alf had a Blitz truck, which carried the supplies out from the Abminga Railway siding, and a jeep. Neither vehicle could negotiate the sand dunes between Indinda Bore and the homestead. In summer I remember the long, hot treks on shanks, toting our suitcases as we'd come home from school in the Alice for the Xmas holidays.

My mother had a magnificent garden at Andado. The place was always ablaze with colourful summer annuals and flowering shrubs. Down around the well and stock tanks she grew an incredible variety of vegetables and melons. In winter we had lawns which lasted until the first summer dust (sand) storm when they'd be covered under a foot of sand. Each winter she dug them out and started again.

Life was extremely hard back then but I remember those days as the best days of my life. We had many adventures. We were marooned by the Finke River near Boundary Bore once—the only bit of dry ground was a rabbit mound and we lived on rabbits for a week. One year we spent Christmas at Boundary Bore when the Finke prevented us from proceeding on home. We suffered a plague of rats that ate everything in sight and we caught up to twenty in rabbit traps in the pantry each night.

Mother sent us to boarding school in the Alice, more for peace of mind than anything else—she was terrified that we might come to grief, as many children did in the bush. To pay the school fees she took advantage of the dingo bounty.

From: Jan Piper, Denman, New South Wales

There was a group of men contracted to build a shed in the town and they were at a loss as to what to do at lunchtime, so they turned to cricket. One of them—Mut Murray—had never played before so they let him bat first because they figured he'd get out quickly and they could get on with the real game. Well, they weren't able to get Murray out on the first day, nor the second day, and by the third day his score was 700 and the blokes had given away the shed and had turned seriously to cricket. In an attempt to get Murray out they changed the rules. They used underarm balls and old tennis balls. They told him that to get a four he had to hit the ball over the fence of a fifty acre paddock and so on. Anyway, on the third day, one of the fielders was smoking during the game and threw his bumper into a pile of eucalyptus tree cuttings. Murray refused to go on batting because the smoke from the burning tree cuttings was too heavy, and he left the crease. At that point the umpire said 'by the powers vested in me by the MCC I declare you dismissed—smoked out'.

From: David Bearup, Guyra, New South Wales

I'm old enough to remember reading *The Bulletin* when it was a real Australian paper. I say that because I reckon that you've brought it back, on the wireless. As the lady says, 'I love it'.

'Cricket at Mum's' brings back real memories for me. I grew up in an inner industrial suburb of Melbourne, Brunswick, had two great yearnings, cricket and the bush. Tried hard at cricket and, as soon as I could, moved to the bush. Trouble with this big country you can't get to live everywhere.

You know, my Mum didn't have a Hills Hoist. We had two wires across the yard with a clothes prop made out of a long, forked tree branch. I reckon I drove the neighbours mad practising batting with a ball hanging from the line. I drove, hooked, glanced and fine cut like Bradman for hours on end, between Sundays that is.

Lived in the Dandenongs, the Otway Ranges and now for about fifteen years in the Barossa. Here we stay on a few acres out of town, looking across at the little village of Bethany and the ranges with Mount Kaiser Stuhl. A great place, strong German character, as most people know, peaceful except at Festival time. I'm a local journo, been writing editorials for about ten years, but I'm now mostly retired so am as busy as ever.

Why do I live here? Well, with forty-eight wineries within fifteen minutes I hardly need any more reasons!

From: Martin Voake, Barossa Valley, South Australia

The first *Australia All Over* book was great, many thanks to you. We were thrilled to see our daughter Margaret's letter published in the 'Testimonials' section.

Having knocked about a bit, every section of your book rekindled many fond memories, particularly the 'Cricket' and 'Trains' sections.

Must tell you about the cricket match we played at Emmet Siding, a railway stop just up from the rail terminus at Yaraka. All the folk for miles around turned up for the dance on the Saturday night in the railway shed. The dance stopped at daybreak in time for a freshen up and brekky prior to the big cricket match out on the clay-pan (middle of January).

The teams were 'Ringers, Fettlers and Shearers' versus 'Squatters, Jackeroos and Ring-Ins'. The latter won the toss and batted first. Nugget, my ringer mate, was opening bowler, dressed, as most of our team was, in 'casual' clobber, that is, ten-gallon hats, shorts, laughin' sides with socks turned down. Well, the opening batsmen made a grand entrance. One was a tall, handsome Pom dressed in old school rig—all whites, pads, gloves, cap, the lot. A most imposing figure of a man. The ladies were most impressed. Nugget, a dead opposite and a Paul Hogan look-alike, was back thirty yards from his wicket end polishing the ball real pro-like and taking it all in.

'Right-e-o', cried the umpy, 'Let 'er rip!'

Well, Nugget streaked across the clay-pan like an emu in oil drums (his little skinny legs protruding from his laughin' sides) and kicking up the dust. When he got to the delivery point he stopped dead and bowled a 'lolly-pop'. I shall never forget it! The ball dribbled down the pitch. Len, the other opening batsman and a jackeroo, surveyed it with utter contempt and casually stepped up to take a swing—missed and was clean bowled middle stump!

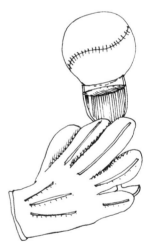

The crowd went wild and so did Len. He threw the willow on the ground and stamped off the field, dismayed, disenchanted and disgusted.

That same day, Choc, a shearer, was fielding. He stepped off the field for a swig of sherry; on his return the batsman got under the ball and lifted it for a sixer. Choc put his hands up and pulled the ball out of the air as it was going over the boundary—the sun was in his eyes at the time! I received a whack in the gob when a ball got through my hands and had to have four top teeth pulled out. I wear a dental plate to this day as a perpetual reminder of that match. It was a most memorable day. We won by ten runs and Nugget was rated as player of the day.

From: Bob Healy, Edi, Victoria

Thank you for your Aussie-flavoured program. We receive it on Sunday evening from 0910 UT in Kota Kinabalu.

I'm living in Kota Kinabalu flying the Fokker 50 for Malaysian Airlines. Why, you ask, is an Australian Airline pilot working for an Asian Airline? Glad you asked. I was one of 1600 pilots involved in the 1989 pilots' dispute, in which 1300 of us lost our jobs. I'd been working for East West Airlines for close to thirteen years and was a relatively senior pilot on the Fokker Friendship based in

Melbourne. I loved the job, serving mainly Tassy ports, Devonport, Wynyard and Hobart. However, in 1989, my Union, the Australian Federation of Air Pilots, decided to take on the companies and Government; we lost badly. About 300 of the 1600 got their jobs back to form the nucleus of the airline system you have today. About seventy-five foreigners, mainly Yanks, took our jobs and are still flying our aircraft.

The whole dispute was a disaster. Although most of us have reapplied to return to Ansett or Australian (now QANTAS), the companies refuse to take us back. We have become permanent outcasts from the aviation scene back home.

It's very hard when a lot of us are overseas without our families and have been so since 1989. A great deal of the remainder have been unemployed since 1989, with their wives supporting the home. A number have committed suicide, unable to handle the rigors of unemployment and marriage break-ups.

So, next time you see Ansett and QANTAS with their pretty little paint jobs, think of the 1300 ex-airline pilots without a job flying at home, trying to hold onto some remnants of Australia and a career.

P.S. I'm trying to write this on a bumpy flight from Kota Kinabalu to Kuala Lumpur.

From: **Captain Bill Hobday, Kota Kinabalu, Malaysia**

IAN TALKS WITH ALEX PIKE, 17 JULY, 1988

What do you in Bunbury, Alex?

ALEX: I'm retired and I spend most of my time up in the goldfields chasing gold.

That's around Kalgoorlie, is it? How often do you do that?

ALEX: Yes, within a radius of approximately a hundred miles of the goldfields. I go up pretty regularly. I've just finished six months up there and I had nine months up in that area, through the Warburton Ranges, back down through the De La Poer encompassing the Victoria and Gibson Deserts.

I don't know what would be better, finding gold or just seeing that country.

ALEX: It's beautiful, Ian. I find it all pleasant and harmonious. The country at the moment is absolutely magnificent with all the wildflowers and the trees in bloom. The fragrance through the bush is beautiful, even up the Canning Stock Route where I made the trip up towards Halls Creek and back again. All the waterholes were full and it was really beautiful.

It sounds lovely, Alex. What are the Warburton Ranges like?

ALEX: They're a little bit dangerous for anybody that doesn't know the country very well. You can get lost quickly unless you've got good compasses and maps and you know where the water is.

Do you drive up there and then go out on foot?

ALEX: Yes. Another chap and I gathered some maps from the Battye Library dating back to the 1890s and we were just chasing old dray tracks. Most of the time we'd walk a couple of miles and then lie down on the ground and pick up the ruts that were grown over—ironstone had blown into them and unless you were lying down you couldn't see them. Then you'd wander through the mulga and find an old mining area and work there for a while.

It must have been really tough when the mines were first put in years ago.

ALEX: Oh, Ian, I've spent a lot of time looking around and you'll see graves in the bush with their names chiselled out onto the stone. Sometimes people have come back and made a proper grave just miles and miles from nowhere. How they found their way through there I'll never know because it's hard enough now with compasses and things like that.

How do you amuse yourself at night when you sit round your campfire?

ALEX: With the accordion or harmonica. It's beautiful, too, because you don't see a soul all day and about ten o'clock at night my little dog will growl and there'll be about half a dozen bush Aboriginals there just sitting and listening, not making a sound. You kick the fire up and draw them in, boil the billy, have a cup of tea, play the mouth organ and they'll sit there, clapping their hands. They're really gentle people in the bush. I feel they're the epitome of communism without the nasties—what's yours is theirs and what's theirs is yours. On several occasions I've tuckered them and a week or so later I'll be miles away and they'll turn up with tea and sugar and bickies and some tobacco then they just disappear again.

119

They must have tremendous hearing, Ian, because you never see them and at night time it's so quiet that the harmonica sound must travel a long way and they pick it up and just wander in quietly and there they are!

Do you get much gold?

ALEX: Sometimes you go up there and get nothing, but last year was good.

And it probably wouldn't matter if you didn't get anything because it sounds like a great lifestyle.

ALEX: I've got a couple of shacks up in the bush and I just move from one to the other when I feel like it. I've got a caravan in one place and my wife comes up and spends a bit of time with me.

I'll come and join you one day and you can take me up to one of your shacks in the bush.

20 JUNE, 1993

I'm going to talk right now to Alex Pike, a mate of ours who first rang the program almost five years ago. Alex is a prospector. How long have you been prospecting, mate?

ALEX: Only since the metal detectors came out in 1978. It fascinated me when I was very young, back in the early 'twenties. Two young chaps were heading for the goldfields and they had this barrow—an enormous board with a big wheel right in the middle and the shaft handles at the front of the back. They had their gear loaded on that and one was pulling, the other was pushing, and they called into our farm to get some food. One played a mouth organ and the other a banjo, and I've always remembered their names—Fred Haig and Charlie Cook. I never saw them again, but when the metal detectors turned up I decided to go out after some gold, just for something to do.

Does it get in your blood? Do you want to find it, make money, find a big nugget?

ALEX: No, it's just the fascination, the challenge to find a piece of gold that's been lying there for millions of years. I keep a lot of it because a nice piece of gold is a collector's item. There are chappies here in Kalgoorlie who do the same thing—they're fascinated with it and they buy specimens, special pieces of gold, and they've bought some of mine. There are some beautiful pieces of gold and you don't like to see them melt it down so I've kept a lot of it, but I sell a lot to tourists, mainly jewellery gold.

Most of the gold leases are owned by the big companies but there are still blokes like you around. How many prospectors do you reckon there'd be around Kalgoorlie—hundreds?

ALEX: Not so much now. There used to be a lot. Back in the late 'seventies or early 'eighties you could still go over the available ground and get gold, but after they came in with the scrapers and things like that it spoiled the alluvial ground completely for anybody prospecting.

Isn't it amazing—people's mad rush for money, money and more money when it really doesn't do you much good, does it? You need enough to have a roof over your head and be comfortable. But you'd have to ask people who are rich—I'm talking about seriously rich people—why they keep wanting more money.

ALEX: It's not so much the money that I do it for, it's the challenge. With the small jewellery gold that's good I photostat the map, mark the area, write when and where the gold was found, sell it to the tourists and tell them to keep it as a family heirloom. That's what I like about gold—it's something for people to have.

During our talk I mentioned a young man by the name of Charlie Cook and his friend, Fred Haig. They were on their way to the north-eastern goldfields in the mid 'twenties. Two days after our talk the telephone rang at home. It was a man named Clarence Charles Cook, Charlie Cook's eldest son. I was stunned! Clarence and his family are on Windsor Station, not far from Mount Magnet in Western Australia.

The next call came from Minlaton, South Australia. It was another son, Jeff Cook! Jeff is a poet and his verse is broadcast on the airwaves.

It's incredible. Charlie Senior only died ten years ago. In such a short time I feel like part of the family and it all came about through *Australia All Over*.

From: Alex Pike, Bunbury, Western Australia

Greetings from Kiwiland! I just had to write and tell you what fun we all had trying to 'play a tune' on a gum leaf! After hearing your program last Sunday and hearing your phone-in guest talk about the Golden Gum Leaf Award—we rushed outside to gather a few leaves and give it a go!

As our radio reception was poor we obviously missed the vital information on how one holds a gum leaf in order to get a tune out of it . . . the smell of eucalyptus filled the kitchen as we all tried various techniques of holding and blowing on the gum leaves. Mother was the first to crack the silence and we went into great roars of laughter as the sound of duck calls filled the kitchen. We never did manage to get a tune from all our efforts, but we sure did have a lot of fun.

Australia All Over is worth getting up early for—'fair dinkum Australiana'! Our family have had a couple of trips to Queensland and had a good look around, as far as Bundaberg to the north and down to Grafton, NSW. We have some great memories of our trips around Australia and hope that maybe one day we will be lucky enough to go over again and see some of our favourite places and explore some new ones!

In the meantime we have your great show to listen to and enjoy! With summer coming up our radio reception should improve!

From: Pam Alphors, Hamilton, New Zealand

Greetings from Chile! I bet you didn't know your program could reach this far! Well, it has—at least via cassette that is. I've been living in Chile for six months and asking my family to 'send some of Macca over', as we used to listen to it every Sunday morning back home. So they did. It was great—loved the songs, the letters you read and long-distance radio and phone calls. Listening to your program I could almost smell the gum trees! In fact I probably could, because there are thousands of them here and wattles too—all of different varieties. Although much drier here, much of the countryside around Santiago looks quite like Australia. My Chilean friends wish there were koalas in the gum trees too.

Life here is very interesting. Happily the economy is booming and on 18th September it will be Chile's Independence Day anniversary, so there will be a lot of celebrations and parades of Huasos (Chilean horseriders) and their magnificent horses as well as Cueca dancing—danced by partners with whirling handkerchiefs.

There is a small Australian contingent here for all number of reasons—work, travel, family reunions etc, and a few of us get together once a month for drinks (after hours) at the Australian Embassy.

Early in the year the Australian and New Zealand community put on a special picnic and fun day at the school I work at, for the Chilean and international families. It was a great day. We were all given 'Bruce' or 'Sheila' badges and we were called that all day. The ladies cooked hard and there were lamingtons and pavlovas galore. Even the barbie was on and cans of New Zealand beer (where was the Fosters?). We had boomerang throwing competitions and gumboot throwing and finished off with a game of cricket—a novelty for many.

So you can see Aussie culture is alive and well here in Chile, although we do mix it a lot with Latin lifestyle.

From: Louise Harrington, Santiago, Chile

I'm not sure how many listeners you have overseas, but now that I have found I can pick up ABC Regional radio on short wave you have at least one more, located at this somewhat isolated mine site in Indonesia. The Kelian gold mine is about 220km inland from the east coast of Kalimantan (that's probably Borneo to you) and is only four kilometres south of the equator. The first gold was produced earlier this year and after the excitement of commissioning, the place is now settling down to a steady routine. The majority of expats up here are from Australia, most working on a six week on, two week off roster. It was one of those going out for his two weeks off who took this letter home with him to post in Australia for me.

When I am at home I usually listen to *Australia All Over* on 3LO in Melbourne. Up here I have been able to pick it up on a Western Australia Regional radio station (The voice of the Northwest) on 15425 kHz. I am not sure where this transmitter is located as I have yet to hear a specific station identification. I can pick up the same station from 06:45 (Western Australia time and ours) each morning during the week (prior to this it appears to be jammed by something). This means I can catch the news at 07:00 (as work starts) and hear a bulletin which gives better coverage of Australian events than the Radio Australia news does.

From: John Waldram in Indonesia

A 'Latin' Lamington

Mary Adams: Obituary
from *The Mudgee Guardian*

One of Gulgong's well-known and respected residents, Mary Adams, passed away on Sunday, February 21, at the Gulgong Hostel at the age of eighty-six. Mary was born on March 18, 1906, to Tom and Adelena Foley. She grew up in Gulgong and was educated at Broadfield School. On July 25, 1928, she married Jack Adams who predeceased her by seventeen years.

They had four children, Vincent, Marie, Betty and Lennie. Mary lived a happy and healthy life. She was one lady who put twenty-five hours into a twenty-four hour day.

One of her many interests was the love of music, in particular her love of her well-known violin.

Mary enjoyed playing for people, even at the ripe old age of eighty-four in a local eisteddfod.

She was proud of being a lifelong resident of Gulgong. She shared her knowledge and experiences with so many people and would never let anyone pass her in the street without her saying hello, or stopping to introduce herself to strangers and sharing with them a little of Gulgong's history.

Mary was also well-known for her Sunday morning chats with Ian McNamara on the ABC's *Australia All Over*.

She certainly made Australians aware of the Town on the $10 note—a place she was proud of.

The last five months she resided at the Gulgong Hostel in poor health, and was lovingly cared for by their staff. As Mary always loved her faith and being with a crowd, it was fitting that on Tuesday, February 23, her funeral was attended by 250 family and friends to say farewell.

She had only one wish left in life and that was fulfilled by having three priests, Father Max Blumental, Father Garry McKeown, and lifetime family friend Father James Collins concelebrate the Requiem Mass. Mary will be sadly missed by her four children, eighteen grandchildren and fourteen great-grandchildren.

From: **Marie Mealing, Gulgong, New South Wales, Mary's daughter**

IAN TALKS WITH SIR HUBERT OPPERMAN

A little treat for us all this morning—I've got Sir Hubert Opperman on the line. He's just ridden through the Sydney Harbour Tunnel. Good morning, Sir Hubert, how are you?

THE QUAMBONE TROMBONES

The famous Quambone trombones. Trying to get a 'tune' out of one of the town's trombones which was built by Simon and Keiren Turnbull.

'What's a big trombone like this doing out here Daph?' It sits at the crossroads just outside of town

I TOOK MY TROMBONE TO TAMWORTH

I took my trombone to Tamworth
But nobody asked me to play
I took my trombone to Tamworth
It just seemed to get in the way
They were pickin' their guitars
And pluckin' their banjos
Singin' about old dogs and beer
And they said "You take your trombone
And go back to Quambone
We don't play your music round here".

When I was a young boy in Quambone
I dreamt one day I'd play guitar
I'd sing through my nose
And wear cowboy clothes
And one day I'd be a star
But there's one thing you learn quick out our way
If music and song is your thing
And that's if you live in Quambone
Then you'll play the trombone
In Quambone the trombone is king

Now Berry has got the big orange
Ballina's got a big prawn
All over Australia big paraphernalia
To most of us just a big yawn
But the tourists won't come past Coonamble
So we all had a think what to do
And the vote was in Quambone
To build a big trombone
You'll see it when you're passing through

Yes I took my trombone to Tamworth
And nobody asked me to play
Yes I took my trombone to Tamworth
It just seemed to be in the way
They were pickin' their guitars
And pluckin' their banjos
Singin' about old dogs and beer
And they said "You take your trombone
And go back to Quambone
We don't play your music round here".
They said "You take your trombone
And go back to Quambone
We don't play that music round here".

Ian McNamara

PEOPLE ALL OVER

Wherever I go listeners ask me about the galah lady, also known as Mary Adams from Gulgong. The galah lady tag came when Mary rang to tell me her galah had died and from these immortal lines:
How long do galahs live, Mary?
I don't know, I'm eighty-four and I'm another galah!

Mary Theresa Adams

Passed away 21st February 1993

Aged 86 years

May she rest in peace

People always complain about not being able to get through to us. Mary must have had a golden dialling finger because she always got through.

SIR HUBERT: Good morning, Macca. If I call you Macca you should call me Oppy, not Sir Hubert.

That's nice—I was going to ask if I could call you Oppy! Did you have a good trip through the tunnel this morning?

OPPY: Oh, it was a magnificent experience, I can tell you. After sixty years going over the Bridge, to go under the water was a terrific experience.

That's right, sixty years ago you cycled across the Bridge. Different times then, Oppy!

OPPY: Yes, but they were exciting, just the same as this morning.

What does the tunnel look like from inside—just another tunnel, I suppose.

OPPY: Well, it was a rather eerie feeling to think that you were cycling under millions of tons of water. I saw a trickle cross the tunnel floor and I quickened my pace immediately.

You still ride, don't you?

OPPY: Oh, yes. I used to go out on the open road, but now the traffic is a bit too thick so I ride for about half an hour a day at the retirement village.

Bike riding was really the big thing fifty or sixty years ago, wasn't it? Bike riders such as yourself were world famous—you were a hero not only to Australians but to people all round the world.

OPPY: Well, it's a great compliment that you've paid me. Mind you, there are more bicycles used today—it's finally broken through to the general public that cycling can be made functional and healthy. That was what I was trying to preach when I was merchandising bicycles with Bruce Small, later Sir Bruce, of the Gold Coast. It does my heart good to see groups and families all enjoying bicycles.

It seems to keep everybody fit, Oppy, doesn't it?

OPPY: My word it does.

How old were you when you first started riding your bike?

OPPY: I was eight years old. I fell for it immediately I saw people on bicycles. From then on I was hooked!

You were a politician for some time. What do you think of politics these days?

OPPY: Well, they've got me confused. The behaviour of parliament and the breaking of protocol such as we knew ... it was rough and tough, but they had ethics. Just as cricket and sport have deteriorated somewhat in sportsmanship so the protocol has been broken countless times with the later generation of parliamentarians, and it grieves me. The standard set by the leaders of the parties in my day, and I'm speaking as an old bloke now, was far above the conduct exhibited now.

So you've never had a hankering to go back—you wouldn't like to be there today.

OPPY: No, once you're out of it ... I will say this: I was in the RAAF for five years and training for and racing in the hardest races in the world—the Tour de France and Paris/Brest/Paris—but the occupation of a politician is one of the most difficult and wearing you could select. After you've been on the platform— 'Opperman the working man' and so on—you feel you've got the responsibility to carry out your undertakings. Even if you split yourself in two you still couldn't do all the work that comes onto your desk from the general public.

Yes, it seems like that. You just mentioned France. You were, and still are, a national hero in France; the crowds used to go berserk over you. A bloke said to me, 'Don Bradman was a great hero, but Opperman was a hero to the world'. How did you cope with that adulation in those days?

OPPY: I was amongst high standard fellows who were winning their classics and I didn't think I stood out that much. A very successful businessman, Bruce Small, was my manager and I had a great affection for him, and he guided me through. If he ever saw me getting above what he thought was my station he'd cut me down to size! I think that was the way I went through life, actually, being pleased with what I did but not being carried away by it. They say that every man has a lurking wish to be thought considerable in his own place; you do get a quiet satisfaction out of winning.

It's lovely to talk to you, Oppy, and congratulations—you've done it again!

Your great conversation with the famous Sir Hubert Opperman brought back memories.

In 1932 I was a student at Woodville District High School, in South Australia. During lunch times, a bunch of us kids used to play 'sticks' in a remote patch of ground. The School Sports Day was in the offing and someone happened to raise the question about the circumference of the school oval, and wondered whether it was more than the 440 yards, which was to be one of the events in the Sports Day to be held at Alberton Oval.

One lad, named Opperman, said 'It's not very far.' Another said 'Oh, yeah? I'd like to see you run around it!' Opperman replied 'I could run around it several times without any trouble!' and offered to do so. The rest of the gang decided to take turns to accompany him to make sure that he did not cut any corners. The first victim was quickly chosen, and he and Opperman set off together. In due course they arrived, Oppy not looking greatly the worse for wear, while his friend dropped to the ground, almost exhausted. Off went Oppy again, with number two. This went on until the bell rang, signalling the end of the luncheon period, by which time Oppy had circled the boundary seven times.

As we trooped into school, Oppy said 'Aw, that was nothing. I could have run around the oval all day. Hubert Opperman is my uncle and all our family are noted for their great lung capacity'. From what we had seen, we certainly had no reason to disbelieve him!

From: **Jack Magnussen, Croydon Park, South Australia**

In 1991 you interviewed both Ivan 'Curley' Lawson and his sister Gladys, the nephew and niece of Henry Lawson, their father being Henry Lawson's younger brother, Peter. Sad to relate, both Ivan and his sister Gladys passed away within nine days of each other quite recently. I am enclosing copies of two obituaries I wrote for our local paper, the *Mudgee Guardian*.

IVAN HERTZBERG LAWSON

An important link with Henry Lawson's Eurunderee was severed last Tuesday when Mr Ivan Hertzberg Lawson died in a Sydney hospital from emphysema. He was seventy-nine years of age.

Last year, June 8, Mr Lawson returned to revisit the old school attended by his father, Peter, and his more famous uncle, Henry—writer of short stories and poems. It was the first time he had been back to the district in over forty years.

His father was born at Eurunderee in 1873 and moved to Sydney in 1883, when Louisa Lawson departed Eurunderee and was later to publish the *Dawn* magazine. Peter Lawson married in 1903 and Ivan (proud of his inherited Hertzberg name) was the eighth of ten children. His eldest sister, Gladys, and younger brother, Albury, survive him.

Ivan Lawson married and had two sons and two daughters, nine grandchildren and three great-grandchildren.

GLADYS LAWSON

Another important link with Henry Lawson country was severed last Thursday, August 6, when Miss Gladys Lawson died in Sydney. She was eighty-four years old.

Nine days previously, on July 28, her brother, Ivan Hertzberg Lawson, predeceased her.

Gladys Lawson was the niece of Henry Lawson, her father being Lawson's younger brother, Peter. Her grandmother was Louisa Albury, the daughter of a Eurunderee pub keeper, who met and married Norwegian sailor Nils Hertzberg Larson during the goldrush in Goldan and Sapling Gullies in the late 1860s.

Miss Lawson was the fourth of ten children and is survived by her younger brother, Albury, who bears his famous grandmother's maiden surname.

Like her grandmother before her Miss Lawson was a woman of determination and independence.

In June 1991 she was scheduled to visit Eurunderee School with her brother Ivan, but was unable to do so for a very good reason. For many years Miss Lawson owned and operated the Wellmaid Cake Shop in West Ryde, renowned for its special fruit cakes. Each Sunday Miss Lawson prepared and soaked fruit for her cakes and any visit to Eurunderee which precluded this ritual could not be contemplated.

Miss Gladys Lawson was buried last Monday at Rookwood Anglican Cemetery, which is also the last resting place of her grandmother.

From: **Norman McVicker, Mudgee, New South Wales**

I was born on March 26, 1923. My father bought the first tractor in the Binya-Barellan district in 1925 when horses were still the main power source on farms. My mother sent me, when I was three or four years old, with morning tea for my father who was working some one-and-a-half miles away. The day was hot and the flies very bad. The long jug of nice, sweet tea had a cloth tied over the top. Of course, I got thirsty on the way and sipped a little tea through the cloth. The further I walked the more I sipped, so you can imagine what I copped when Father removed the cloth to reveal an empty jug!

In 1931, the middle of the Depression, Father paid a deposit on a one-and-a-half tonne Chevrolet truck. I was as proud as punch when he showed me the name on the truck door—J H O'Brien, Carrier. My name! I didn't realise it then, but with creditors everywhere it wasn't wise to register the truck in his name.

In 1932-33 my father and the family left the farm and he opened a garage in Binya (he was a tradesman). I was ten and up until then had only had a total of one year's schooling, including riding a horse for ten miles to and from school for three months. After starting school in Binya I missed an average of two days each week. The Depression was still on and my father found it extremely hard to keep a wife and six kids. I was the eldest and hired labour was out of the question.

At the age of eleven, at wheat carting time, I dragged the bags to the side of the truck with bag hooks. My father reached down and with some aid from me hauled them onto the truck. The next year I was able to lay a bag down and lift the rest onto it. By the age of thirteen or fourteen I was driving the truck on my own. When I was fifteen Father bought another truck. What a monster! It had a twelve-foot tray and carried a mighty eighty bags of wheat. I drove the Chev and my father the monster. When eventually I went to the Police Station for a driving licence the Sergeant said, 'But you've been driving round Binya for years!'

The earliest school-leaving age was fourteen. Two weeks before the exams my father said I could take a fortnight off from helping him at the garage and study. 'If you pass, I'll give you £25.' So, I studied hard, easily passed the exam, got the £25 and bought a £20 cool safe for Mum!

Some childhood memories from J H O'Brien, Tathra, New South Wales

So, David Fleay has left us, that kind, gentle man who was so firm in his beliefs. A man who loved trees and birds and animals and children, greatly honoured in zoological circles as the first man to encourage a number of Australian native animals and birds to breed in captivity—the platypus and the powerful owl, just for starters. Did you know he took an owl to university with him when he was an undergraduate, and in consequence drew many protests from his fellow students when it hooted at night and disturbed their slumbers? David loved owls and tamed many of them. There was one he used to take to lectures he gave in Melbourne—it used to ride on the back of the front seat next to his ear and they used to hoot amiably to each other. Once at a traffic light another motorist pulled alongside just as David said 'Hoot Hoot' to the owl and the owl said 'Hoot Hoot' back to him. The motorist took off as though all the devils in hell were after him!

Along with Judith Wright, Kathleeen Macarthur and my old boss, Brian Clouston, he helped call the foundation meeting of the body which became the Queensland Wildlife Preservation Society. One of my joys at visiting his wonderful West Burleigh sanctuary was the cage he had of sulphur-crested cockatoos. Quite often when an elderly relative died and was outlived by a pet cockatoo the relatives would take the bird to David and ask him to give it a home. He had quite a number of these, about fiteen at one stage, and as all of them had some kind of vocabulary (and perhaps learned from one another?) a visit to their cage was very entertaining. In a way, one heard the voices of the dead because all the birds had been taught by their former owners. There was one ancient, almost bald corella who would sidle along the perch if you spoke to it, place its wrinkled blue cheek against the wire mesh and say in an old, very cultivated lady's voice 'Haven't you got a cup of tea?' My kids loved it and my wife, Mavis, immortalised its question in her children's book *Birdstone Summer*.

From: Bill Scott, Warwick, Queensland

Here's Bill Scott again:

What a beaut program from Boulder! I did enjoy it so much. This might have been because I'm an old gully-scratcher myself, of course; in fact I still carry a dish and a little number one round-nose shovel and a prospector's hammer in the boot of the old Falcon just in case the urge strikes me when I'm crossing a likely-looking creek! Not that the drought we are having has given me any scope this past couple of years—most creeks are dry.

Listening to Alex Pike talk about the charm of prospecting made me think. It's so true what he said. When you are looking for the elusive colour it's possibly not with the intention of getting rich quickly at all, though that would perhaps be nice enough. No, it's the metal itself—it's so beautiful to see; and to find a nugget, even a small one, is a thrill that can't be described. It's something that has been in existence for uncounted millions of years; it doesn't rust or deteriorate. Truly it is called 'the noble metal'.

My wife Mavis once said to me, 'What would you do if ever you did find a really big strike?' I couldn't answer her, of course. My thinking had never reached that far. Maybe Robert Louis Stevenson was right when he said it was better to travel hopefully than to arrive. It's the search itself that gets you in; the endless debates you have with yourself about what might have happened to make the rocks twist and lie the way they do, where the little specks might have come from, their source and what might have happened to spread them the way they are, where they came from and whether it might be possible to trace their path.
(*The interview with Alex Pike is on page 118.*)

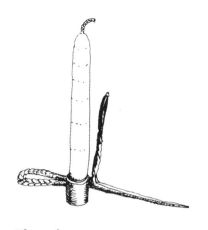

Miner's Candleholder

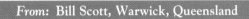

From: **Bill Scott, Warwick, Queensland**

The Australian explorer Donald Mackay was born near Yass, New South Wales, in 1870. In 1899 he rode a bicycle around Australia on a trip which lasted 240 days, and following that did much inland exploration of the remote central and northern regions of Australia. In 1926 he went to the Peterman Ranges with a camel team, in 1928 to Arnhem Land on horseback and between 1930 and 1937 he completed four aerial survey trips, covering the inland again. Trips were made from base camps at Fitzroy, Tanami, Wave Hill, Cook, Forrest, Rawlinna, Laverton, Docker and Hermannsburg. During these survey trips Donald Mackay discovered several new lakes, including Lake Jubilee. Lake Mackay on the Western Australian and Northern Territory border was named in his honour. Mackay gave copies of all his maps and reports to the Australian Government and the Mitchell Library in Sydney. It seems none of his trips were sponsored financially by the Government.

From: **Ruth Hill, Dickson, Australian Capital Territory**

My father used to talk about Donald Mackay a lot and I got the impression one knew the other quite well.

Donald Mackay lived in Cronulla and his house is still standing. When I was a child, before the war, and we would go out in our boat from Burraneer Bay we would pass the house. It was a brown weatherboard house with a shingle roof. Before the war it stood on a large parcel of land and was waterfronted, but with the land subdivision it now stands surrounded by many houses with other homes between it and the water. In about 1982 it had its centenary.

From: **Elva Carmichael, Tuncurry, New South Wales**

As program manager for heritage for the Australian Institute of Cartographers, I have researched something of the history of mapping in Australia and presented a paper on the Donald Mackay aerial surveys.

Mackay did not pioneer aerial survey in Australia. This honour goes to Gerald Halligan who took aerial photos of Lake Eyre in 1922.

Donald Mackay was not knighted, though he did receive a CBE. He was a kind of 'Dick Smith', an adventurer, who financed his own expeditions. He received practically no help from the Government, only hindrance. Yet the four Mackay aerial surveys, with a very small party and at no cost to the Government, produced maps covering about a quarter of the continent. While these maps were primitive by today's standards they were better than anything available up to that time.

I believe that Donald Mackay was a remarkable man who deserves some recognition. The bike on which he did his record breaking round Australia trip is on display at the Powerhouse Museum.

From: John McCarthy, Sydney, New South Wales

We were a group of three couples travelling home from the Birdsville Races via Innamincka.

We camped on Cooper's Creek near Innamincka one night then did the tourist attractions visiting the site where Wills died, the site where Grey was rescued, the site where Burke died and the Dig Tree the next day.

On first sighting the beautiful big lagoons of the Cooper, presumably full of fish, and the plentiful birdlife, we declared we could not understand why men died here of starvation.

By the time we had trudged through hot sand and one of our husbands had nigh choked to death on a fly, the Cooper was beginning to pall.

As the sun rose higher and the flies became so thick we were battling to get a spoonful of lunch from our plates to our mouths without all choking to death, and paddling in the Cooper afforded little respite from flies and heat, the place became oppressive.

When we erected our small tents about a kilometre from the Dig Tree and the wind blew so hard we had to shift them to better shelter——we were fed up with the place. And this was only three o'clock in the afternoon. How those poor men lasted as long as they did is anyone's guess! Aside from any other consideration, however, they did make one glaring mistake——*They didn't take any women to tell them what to do.* This became perfectly obvious to our blokes.

Weren't they lucky they had us girls to whack them on the back when they were choking? Weren't they lucky they had us there to tell them how and where to erect the tents—once, twice or however many times they had to be done per day in the wind? Weren't they lucky they had us there to insist they drove in a certain direction when they became disorientated and wanted to go the wrong way in the desert?

I'm glad they are recognising pioneer women, Ian. There must have been so many who saved their blokes from ruination. We know—we're still doing it!

From: Avril Annett, Wangaratta, Victoria

Recently I called you from a public telephone near Jupiter Well.

No doubt using latest Telecom technology, it is solar-powered and linked by a series of microwave towers through other Aboriginal communities to Alice Springs. Nowhere could you have a more tranquil setting for a public telephone—looking out through a stand of beautiful desert oak trees and low, spinifex-covered sand dunes.

This phone was set up for the new Nyinmi Aboriginal Outstation, which at the time of our visit was not occupied. It is part of a government program responding to Aboriginal interest in returning to their homelands, in this case the Bindubi people.

My wife and I worked at Warburton and Docker River Aboriginal communities in the 1970s and made several treks out through this area, a quite remote part of the Great Sandy Desert. You could probably imagine my surprise this year when in the same area we came across a group of steel-framed huts, shower blocks and a public telephone! We had driven down from Kununurra, via Halls Creek, Balgo Community and Lake Mackay, joining the east-west track at Mt Webb. This runs for about 600 kilometres from Papunya past Jupiter Well to Gary Junction. The well was sunk in 1962 by surveyors from the Division of National Mapping to provide water for teams in a major survey project.

After our memorable Jupiter Well camp we called at Well 33 on the Canning Stock Route to replenish our water supplies, then headed south.

Just to prove the extent to which bush people tune in to *Australia All Over*, two weeks and 2100 K later our two four-wheel drive vehicles passed through Seemore Downs station near Rawlinna on the Transcontinental Railway. The family there was expecting us as they had heard our call from Jupiter Well.

From: David Hewitt, Tumut, New South Wales

These are the words of my song about a 'famous person'.

READ ME LITTLE BOOK

Ah, g'day,
I've got a little tip for you.
Like a good read
Yeah, I thought you did.

You know I got the elbow from the party years ago
And I can hear 'em laughin' at me everywhere I go;
But I'm gonna have the last laugh, my friend.
Now go and take a look
At the great Australian novel
Yeah—Hawkie's little book

Yeah, read it in me book,
Yeah, I went and wrote a book
I tell ya what, there's a few round town
Who are feelin' pretty crook.
It's not that I'm vindictive, and I wouldn't hurt a chook,
But what went on and who said what—
It's all there in me book.

Ah, yeah, it's a beauty, mate.

Now the narrative goes everywhere like a feral shoppin' trolley
And it's written by this gambling former alcoholic pollie (that's me!)
And in this book, fair dinkum, I come out smellin' like a dahlia,
While Paul, he comes out smelling like his description of Australia!

(Read it in me book—anyway don't believe me)

Yeah, go and buy the book.
Hazel's in there, Richo too,
It's worth a flamin' look.
And you'll see all the flak I copped,
The trouble that I took.
I'll be surprised if you don't buy ten—
Yeah, read it in me book
(Wonder if 60 Minutes want me?)

Now honesty and integrity weren't words used by Ned Kelly
But you'll hear them often in this book and on the telly (g'day, Jana!)
But if everything that's in here isn't gospel, mate, the best,
Well, blow me down, I'll take a flamin' lie detector test.

Read me little book.
Yeah, go on, go and buy the novel
The greatest thing since Shakespeare, that's all,
Covers more ground than Hume and Hovell.
And you know I wouldn't dud ya, so take a Captain Cook
At me modest little effort
Yeah, go and read me book.

Talks . . . And if ya had the intellect and the integrity and
the education then I wouldn't have to keep tellin' ya—
Go and buy it! Help me pay for the house and the dish.
Ya seen the dish? Ah, yeah, it's great. I have a bet now
and again. You have a bet yourself, do ya? Yeah, why don't
ya come over? Chippy comes over, Singo . . . A few of us get
together and have a bit of a bet. But before ya come over
I'd strongly advise ya to . . .

Read me little book
Go and grab the book.
I tell ya what, there's a few round town
Who are feelin' really crook.
It's not that I'm vindictive, and I wouldn't hurt a chook,
But what went on, and who said what—
Yeah, it's all there in me book.

Ah, go and buy it. I'm working on the sequel now!

I can't believe that whoever wrote the song, 'Read My Little Book' (very good;
was it you, we missed the credits?) had not heard the following limerick which
is most appropriate even down to the 'Westralian'. This is it, anyway:

> There was a young man from Westralia,
>
> Who painted his bum like a dahlia,
>
> The colours were true—
>
> Red, white and blue—
>
> But the smell of the flower was a failure.

I did not know that the former PM was interested in gardening. Perhaps after he has completed his literary efforts and given his former colleagues a working over he should turn his attention to horticulture. One can imagine him entering a prize bloom at the Royal Agricultural Flower Show in due course with this pedigree:

Section:	Faded blooms
Class:	Deteriorating
Specimen:	Dahlia vitriolus
Breeding:	Dahlia Hawkensis crossed by (not with)Dahlia Keatinginiana.

NB   This specimen is now of historical interest only and is not recommended for further breeding or for display for its appearance or aroma.

From: **Geoff Armstrong, Lake Cathie, New South Wales**

THAT SONG

Hello Macca, we are writing
Re your new song most exciting,
With its mention of Bob's book and PM Paul,
And the story somewhat slighting,
Of indelicate back-biting
Which is sure to start an interesting squall.

And though sleep you were defying
It would seem there's no denying
That the end result was worth a loss of sleep;
There's no doubt we'll all be buying
Bobby's book . . . so edifying,
So that we behind the scenes may take a peep.

And now Bob is prophesying
That the PM's star is dying
And a gent with other views will take his job . . .
That the Polls are signifying
Changed opinions gratifying
Both for Alexander Downer and for Bob.

Well done Ian, it's a beauty!

From: **Jim and Dorothy Watt, Briagolong, Victoria**

136

THE PEOPLE'S POETRY

If I was asked what's the national sport, I'd have to say writing poetry. Australians continue to write poetry of all sorts, good and bad, in books, on home computers. Most of it finds its way to my office and I try to read a couple of poems every week. I think poetry must be remembered and recited to be effective. It's not much good sitting on a page. My favourite poem of the moment is 'Verandahs' by the late Bob Brissenden.

Pauline Smart from Port Augusta in South Australia wrote this poem under the pen name Josephine Thomas. It's a little beauty and speaks volumes for rural women. Bushmen and farmers, raise your hats to them:

A RURAL WOMAN

Things are different now that the season's dry,
And the market's down, and the staff has gone.
The poor sheep don't know though,
Heads down, creamy oblongs stringing in to water,
Worth less than the feral goats in the hills.

The colours of the land become more vivid
With each dry day,
And even the shade seems hotter.
The icing on the Christmas cake
Will melt again this year.

Dusty legs, bare feet, my son rushes in
For water and a hug.
Some hard playing with the old sheep dog.
Watch for snakes, won't you mate!
Starting school over the radio next year.

I glance at my belly, eight months rounded,
And hope again
I don't have it here in the kitchen,
Next to the Flying Doctor radio,
I smile at the thought of my husband helping.

He's one of the things that's different now,
He used to be cheerful and bluff and tired.
Now he's short-tempered and restless and weary.
He deserves more than just
Work-socks for Christmas. He's only thirty.

I stare at the place where my garden should have been.
The salty bore-water has won, as it has with my skin,
And my hair and my clothes.
But at least the bark chips, carefully laid
Will keep the dust down.

And sometimes I long for coffee and a chat
With a girlfriend, and to giggle.
A holiday, a perm, a spending spree,
A swim, a meal at a restaurant,
God forgive me, a babysitter.

I'm tired of the news in the papers and journals,
And of feeling like a doll
In the back of a politician's wagon.
Thank goodness we only get mail once a week,
So I miss most of what they say.

And I feel like lying down.
Cheek against this red earth,
Taking comfort, trusting it.
It's easier to accept what it gives.
At least it never makes any promises.

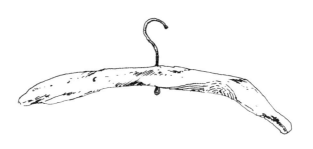

ON McCAFFERTY'S RUN

You must go down to McCafferty's
One Friday evening at four
And mix with the crowd, that is milling around
You can barely get inside the door

Now there's Sally who's going to Wee Waa
And Richard who's on a long haul
There's Jenny and Mick, whose Nanna is sick
So they'll get off the bus at Blackhall

And I'm on my way down to Melbourne
Cause my Golden One's thirty on Sunday
Would she hold on a tick, if I took a quick trip?
I could probably make it by Monday!

I could pop up the road to Mt Isa
And stop on the way at Cloncurry
Explore Tennant Creek, and be back in a week
Then hop on the bus to the Murray

Or maybe I'll go up to Emerald
And then out to Longreach by noon
Visit 'The Hall', make a telephone call
And tell them 'I'll be there real soon'

Or maybe we'll go through Wilcannia
It shouldn't take all that long
And have morning tea, where the Darling runs free
Then stop off at Shepparton

They tell me it's wet in Echuca
And the river is rising fast
Perhaps we will stop, until there's a drop
And then on to Melbourne at last

On McCafferty's wall in Toowoomba
The menu is clearly on show
One day I'll come back, with my back-pack
And it's off to 'The Olgas' I'll go

I scurry on out from the depot
And seek out the Melbourne queue
What glorious fun, ON McCAFFERTY'S RUN
I'll come back to this place, wouldn't you?

From: **Helen Fielding, Kingscliff, New South Wales**

ALL STOPS OUT

Up here in New England, (I think it's just for fun),
We've got a heap of 'STOP' signs, for trains that used to run,
The Great Northern Railway, is a sad and sorry tale,
For trains no longer run, North of Armidale.
But with typical bureaucracy, that no one can define,
If you want to cross the idle tracks, you must obey the sign,
They've auctioned all the houses off, demolished quite a few,
Their fences all are tumbledown and signals lie askew.
The 'Griffiths Bros' tea signs, with miles to go are gone,
Once well tended station gardens, are struggling, pale and wan,
Just a few crossing gates lie tangled in the grass,
Memories of urchins perched atop, cheering trains that passed.
Now here's a list of 'STOP' signs, as best I can recall,
There's sure to be some mistakes, I won't have got them all,
Starting near the Uni, on the old Bundarra Road,
Two more to Dumaresq, where once the 'phosphate flowed,
There's Exmouth and Black Mountain, where the station's beautified,
A local interest group have helped to stem the tide,
Climbing up to Guyra, 'Mother of Duck's Lagoon' abeam,
A major watering stop, in the long lost days of steam.
Four Crossings to Llangothlin, where they loaded spuds and peas,
Buildings have all gone now, memories in the breeze,
Two more to Ben Lomond, which is as high as you can go,
Lofty 5000 feet, have seen their share of ice and snow,
Down hill to Glencoe, Red Lion Tavern on the right,

AUSTRALIAN SIGNS

There's only one country in the world where you'll find phone boxes and road signs like these! David Hewitt called the program from a phone box beneath the tree on Nyinmi Aboriginal Outstation near Jupiter Well, 850 km from Alice Springs; they may not be pretty but there's no denying the signs tell you all you need to know.

ANDADO STATION

These photographs by Barry Skipsey show us broadcasting from the old and very remote Andado Station which is about 370 km from Alice Springs. The waddy tree is one of the rarest trees on this earth.

Train crews stopped to sip, then thundered through the night.
Over the highway at Stonehenge, with granite rocks around,
Almost into Glen Innes, where STOP signs do abound,
It's Deepwater, Bolivia, then Tenterfield my friend,
I've just run out of stations, we've come to journeys end.
That's an awful lot of crossings, though I haven't kept a score,
I'd have a guess at forty, maybe there's several more,
So Mr Commissioner for Railways, I reiterate again,
Come and get your stop signs, or give us back a train.

From: David Bearup, Guyra, New South Wales

ONLY TOURISTS NOW

Innamincka, Birdsville,
Channel country towns,
Surrounded by red claypans,
And shiny stony downs,
Exotic sounding place names,
Dust ridden and bleak,
Clinging to the stock route,
Along the Cooper Creek,

Conjure up lean drovers,
Cattle feeding by,
Endless rows of sandhills,
Stretching to the sky,
Five hundred miles to travel,
Through a desert hell,
To reach the southern market,
By waterhole or well.

But if you visit nowdays,
It's not like that at all,
You'll never see the stock route,
Drovers riding tall,
Or any sign of ringers,
Boozing up a cheque,
Horses waiting quietly,
Hobbles round their neck,

Just one or two old buildings,
The pub and AIM,
And houses, neatly painted,
You'll see a swag of them,
Antiseptic little boxes,
As interesting as dirt,
With the nearest thing to colour,
Some old black man's shirt.

The people walking Main Street,
Won't be bushmen and their wives,
But long socked collared gentry,
From the 4-wheel drives,
That cluster round the bowsers,
Waiting to depart,
Once the drivers and their families,
Have checked the super-mart.

For souvenirs and postcards,
To let their friends all know,
They made it to the outback,
Where but the hardy go,
And as they face the desert,
With an icecream in each fist,
They head home feeling certain,
There was nothing that they missed.

But I was still there dreaming,
In my humpy up the back,
If they'd driven off the main road,
And up the bumpy track,
And could have shown pack bags,
Saddles, all the gear,
Left over from the horse plant,
I sold that final year.

When I realised the road trains,
Had made us obsolete,
As I brought the last walked cattle,

Down that Thompson beat,
And could have told some stories,
Of those rough days long gone,
But they don't have time to visit,
They're too, eager to move on.

Tales about the dry stage,
Four days without a drink,
Ninety miles to push them,
From Reids to Hallett's sink,
Camping on a sandhill,
Stranded there for weeks,
As Queensland rains come flooding,
Down the Cooper's creeks . . .

The Publican's a towny,
But we get on rather well,
And we often exchange glances,
As we listen as they tell,
How the track was rough and stony,
And the two spare tyres blew,
Done it tough along the Cooper?
They wouldn't have a clue!

From: **Geoff Allen, Balgowlah, New South Wales**

A SLEEPY LIZARD DAY

New growth on tall gums
gleams on the roadside
on a warm Australian morning
already this Sunday has become
a sleepy lizard day—
a day for adventuring
with lizards slowly crawling
over warm bitumen
gambling their lives
to cross to yakkas on the other side
where flowering yakkas

point like spears
towards a wide, blue sky

a sleepy lizard reaches
the other side
where the grass is greener
blue tongue flicking and tasting the breeze
his skin shining in the sunlight

he moves faster
thrilled by golden dandelions
he enters a lizard's paradise
with strong jaws he chomps on perfect petals
there are so many to choose from
but his table manners are such
you'd hate to dine with him in a restaurant

when footsteps approach
he escapes through the grass
in a strange four legged run
he stole from a carpet of gold,
and has now become
surprise surprise
the fastest sleepy on the ground.

From: Joy Broughton, Port Lincoln, South Australia

THE MAN FROM SHEEPWASH CREEK

For Weary Dunlop

He packed his kit and he went to war
With the eighth division to Singapore,
And many a tear slid down the cheeks
For the fine young man from Sheepwash Creek.

With their guns ablaze, and bayonets drawn,
The battle raged in the early dawn
And the medico they went to seek
Was a tried and true from Sheepwash Creek.

Far from the land of the blossom gum,
The enemy marched them one by one
To a camp where no one dared to speak—
'Cept the spirited man from Sheepwash Creek.

And their hell was called the Burma trail—
With skeletal frames they built the rail,
While their blessed saviour—so to speak—
Was the medical man from Sheepwash Creek.

The medical man with the weary eyes,
He watched 'em bleed and he watched 'em die.
He batted on with the sick and weak—
Did the weary man from Sheepwash Creek.

But it's now I hear the bugle sound,
A last hurrah for the heaven bound.
And a million tears roll down the cheeks.
Good-bye, good shepherd, from Sheepwash Creek.

From: **Heather Prentice, Hawks Nest, New South Wales**

AN HONEST DAY'S WORK
OR THE AUSSIE ETHIC

Oh God it'd be good
To have an honest day's work
With sweat on your brow
And dirt on your shirt.
The evening meal
Would go down with zest
Instead of just sitting
Like a lump in your chest.
You might have a beer
Knowing well that it's earned.
Never thought for hard labour
One day I would yearn,
A good hot shower

145

Washes dirt down the drain
No tired aching muscles
I refuse to complain,
I might go out bowling
In a fresh pair of socks
I'd have spending money
No need for 'The Box'.
And when I laid down
I'd go straight off to sleep
The wife and the kids
No worry to keep.
And when it came payday
Wouldn't seem like a lurk
Oh God it'd be good
To have an honest day's work!

From: Clem J Collier

THE DYING REQUEST

Patrick was laying upon his death-bed
His life-long friend Michael stood there near his head
His heart full of sorrow a tear in his eye
He knew Pat was going to that big pub in the sky

'Michael,' said Patrick, 'There's one last request
'Which I'd like to make before I'm laid to rest.'
'Why say it,' said Michael, 'y'know I'm the man
'That would willingly do it if any man can.'

'In yonder wee cupboard, behind the white bowl
'There's a bottle of whusky that's fifty years old
'And thro' years o' temptation that bottle I've saved
'Now I want you t'pour it all over me grave.'

'T'pour it,' said Michael, 'My God! What a waste,
'All over the ground without even a taste.'
'But Michael, old pal, it's me dyin' request.
'Please tell me ye'll do it 'fore I'm laid t'rest.'

'Yer dyin' request? Why sure Patrick for you,
'I'll do it, but Pat I've a last request too.
'The sight o' this whusky has brought on a thirst
'Would y'mind if I passed it through my kidneys first?'

Now Pat's eyes were closed when Mike spoke his last word
And nobody knows if his old friend had heard.
Pat quietly expired and no answer he gave
So Michael did faithfully pee on his grave.

From: **Charles Devine, Castlemaine, Victoria**

MY COUSIN AL

My cousin Al, in New South Wales, sent me a Christmas box
Not Vegemite (of which I'm fond) nor my favorite fancy chocs,
But *Australia All Over*—McNamara's masterpiece.
Well Done! Abou Ben, Ian! and may your tribe increase!

Would you kindly mention Normanton among your future talks?
No! Not that one in Queensland—The Pommie one, in Yorks
'Cause Al and I both hail from there, but he left long ago
To settle down in New South Wales. (Well, someb'dy had to go!)

As good a place as Normanton you'd find it hard to get,
So I've harvested a Money-tree, to visit Oz—by Jet—
Where, God willing, after all those years I'll do the best I can
To down a drink with dear old Al—in Coona-bara-bran!

From: **Frank Geeson, Normanton, Yorkshire, England**

147

THEY'RE PINCHING OUR RAIN

Day after day we gaze with
eyeballs glued to the weather map
wavy bands of isobars
rain approaching from the west

But lo and behold before our unbelieving eyes
our beautiful bands retreat once more
they've slipped away, they've disappeared
to hover over southern shores

In Tassie, Melbourne and Kiwiland
they're up to their knees in mud
we'd cheerfully give their lives a lift
and lend them a bit of our sun

While our gumbooted southern neighbours
are squelching in glorious mud
we're staring at our sunbaked paddocks
please give those isobars the shove

We know you're decent folk at heart
and wouldn't harm a fly
and you'll never hear us complain again
if you'll just stop pinching our rain

From: Betty Culver, Hivesville, Queensland

THIRTY-FIVE YEARS I WORKED AS A COCKY

Thirty-five years I worked as a cocky
And ran a bush business to boot
My grownup kids have got it all now
Let them have the worry and loot.

I flew for a while to the stations
But now I've the life of a rover

We take our home wherever we go
Macca: 'It's Australia All Over'.

From Perth up the coast to the tropics
See the Kimberley rugged and rough
Camp in a gorge and catch a fish
You get some but never enough.

It's taken six months to get round it
And we're keen to start off again
Our camper is one that can go anywhere
From the mountains to coastal plain.

We have camped by a crocodile river
Seen the desert grow out of the dawn
A rain forest run right down to the sea
And grass stretch away like a lawn.

There's lakes that appear in the goldfields
Been through water a metre deep
After twenty-six inches of soaking rain
When seven's 'bout average for sheep.

So Macca, g'day from WA
We've heard you from Broome to the 'Brook
Was given your book for me birthday
To read when reception is crook!

From: Bob Batchelor, Claremont, Western Australia

ODE TO 'I'M ON A COMMITTEE'

Oh, give me your pity,
I'm on a committee,
Which means that from morning to night,
We attend, and amend, and contend, and defend,
Without a conclusion in sight.
We confer and concur,
We defer and demur,

149

And reiterate all of our thoughts,
We revise the agenda with frequent addenda,
And consider a load of reports.
We compose and propose, we suppose and oppose,
And the points of procedure are fun,
But through various notions and brought up as motions,
There's terribly little gets done.

From: Brian Powell, Toowoomba, Queensland

THE O-TWO TRIPLE-THREE TEN-TWENTY LAMENT

I tried to ring you, Macca,
Like you tell us all to do.
I wanted to talk about lots of things,
But, no good! I couldn't get through!

I wanted to tell you about the frogs
In the Fitzgerald Park in May:
We couldn't drive in to Twertup
'Cause it rained all the previous day.

So we camped in a shearers' quarters,
And went out on the back of a ute
With torches strapped to our foreheads.
It was cold, but rugged-up, it was beaut.

We found gilgies with eyes like rubies on stalks,
Lots of frogs on the edge of the soak:
It takes some skill to catch them,
But you can name them by their croak.

On the Calyerup Rocks in the moonlight
Like magic it was, it's true.
So I rang you to tell you about it,
But, you know, I couldn't get through!

Tree frog singing

150

Then I hoped to describe the eclipse of the moon
We watched from our house down here:
It rose and hung like a smoky pearl,
Incredibly lovely and clear.

And I wanted to talk about three humpback whales
Below in the bay, silver-blue.
They were diving and blowing and snorting,
But . . . no luck! I couldn't get through!

I wanted to tell you of so many things
We see, living where we do:
Of orchids and bush rats and eagles,
But, no use! I just couldn't get through!

So when I woke early this morning
And a rhyme came into my head,
I thought I'd write this and send it by FAX,
And you could read it instead!

From: **Priscilla Broadbent, Bremer Bay, Western Australia**

BEYOND THE SPINIFEX

Beyond the spinifex
Time has no meaning
Out there a man is always on his own
Depending on the kind of life he's seeking
Or if the bush is where he likes to roam
He could be just a drifter from the city
Tired of the task of waiting for the dole
Who's searching for a dream that's non-existent
A man who's lost all hope of any goal
He could be passing through
Perhaps a drover
Who's restless like the cattle on the run
Who likes the thrill he gets from new horizons
Of pitching camp, when all his work is done
He could be some old swaggie, just a loner

An old bloke who is well beyond his prime
Who loves the bush and all it has to offer
No need to hurry, he has lots of time
It could be shearers heading from the mulga
The shearer doesn't mind a life that's rough
He wouldn't swap this life for any other
And as for city life, he's had enough
Beyond the spinifex the roads unending
If freedom is the thing you're searching for
It's there in every creek, in every valley
Your search is over, stay and search no more.

From: Dulce Jones, Newcomb, Victoria

MACCA'S ON THE PHONE

The calls come in from all over the world
Events, anniversaries—all are unfurled,
It's Sunday morning and Macca's on the phone
On *Australia All Over*—we are never alone.

Put pen to paper—tell Macca what you did when you turned off your TV.
We had a call to tell us Flo and Reg have been married seventy-one years in 1993.
Trish from Katherine rang looking for some rain,
And in WA the square dance convention is on once again.
Operation Hammer—now what the hell is that?
Macca wasn't allowed in and he only wanted a chat.

Now Tim the spruiker—boy he's really been around,
Told us that in side show alley people get knocked out every round.
And Tim got confused—thought that Fred had lost his thumb,
When in reality—some one had pinched Fred's drum.

Buy in your own home town—that's where the business should stay.
Hey, seven-year-old Nancy rang to wish us a Happy Father's Day.
A hundred towns with double names were dropped right in our lap,
And after the platypus talk—Tassie told us they were again left off the map.

Lisle rang from the Bakery in Mungindi—but now here's the rub,
He was off to Quambone for a BBQ at the pub.
The rear gunner in Yorkshire rang to dodge the dinner speeches,
The Mayor of Leeton rang and said buy plenty of Letona Peaches.

How about the 107-year-old who is keeping her head above water,
Whilst being looked after by her eighty-year-old daughter.
Dogs and rings were lost and Macca got the blame,
A bloke rang from New Guinea telling us golf was his favourite game.
The bloke rang from Ross Island where it was twenty-eight below,
And the bloke pushing the barrow round is still well on the go.

Roger, the tree man, now he's nobody's fool,
He comes to town every time there's a reunion at a school.
The Trek Back man was told to take a tie to Cairns,
A bloke rang from Bowen to say fog was holding up the vans,
He told us all to eat a banana every morning,
And we hear about capsicums in salads—received a timely warning.

Daylight saving is on again and causing a lot of fuss,
Did you know that a water rat and wandering duck started off the platypus.

The footy finals are finished, and the winners we do laud,
But all the bloody footballs were imported from abroad.
Ah well, I suppose it really takes all types
Next year we want the anthem played on Macca's bag pipes.

Macca's still on the phone, talking the program through,
I'm gonna try to get on—how about you?

From: Col White, Innisfail, Queensland

WHEN WE FINALLY BECOME A REPUBLIC

When we finally become a republic,
When we've given tradition the shove,
And we look for a new type of leader
Of this wide open land that we love,

153

A person who cares for our country,
Sees the good and the bad at first hand,
Who knows what is happening around us,
And sees how it's ruining our land.
You can keep Keating, Hewson and Howard,
And Button and Dawkins and Packer,
I'll vote for the one who is part of our lives;
Our own one and only Ian Macca!!

From: Ron Strahan, Sofala, New South Wales

ROB

Light snowballs on the ranges
Wasn't what she meant to say
So Ian, being helpful,
Tried hard to save the day.

Insects sap the suck
Wasn't what she meant to scribble
But Ian couldn't let it pass
And gave us all a giggle.

Sunday breakfast at the café
Is where we like to meet,
Everything expensive
Is what she likes to eat.

Neville has been anxious
To look at Robyn's style,
He's been hoping for a photo
And waiting quite a while.

Robyn we all love you,
Your giggles make us glow,
So while Ian takes a well-earned rest
Won't you stay and run the show?

From: Anony Mouse

IAN TALKS WITH BILL FORDYCE
7 NOVEMBER 1993

BILL: Because of your interest in trombones, I thought you'd be interested in hearing this. I was a prisoner of war in Stalagluft 3 in Germany during the war, and the men used to soak raisins, kohlrabi skins, potato peelings and sugar in a big German bath and make a very rough red wine. One day an Englishman came into the camp, and said, 'Look, we should distil this', and he found that a German jam tin was a press fit onto the bugle end of a trombone. So he used to boil up the red wine in the jam tin, wrap wet socks around the coils of the trombone, and out of the mouthpiece, onto which he put a rubber tube, he got 98% proof alcohol, and whenever I hear you on your trombone I think, well, I don't like your music much but I really go for the trombone because of its benefits other than playing! It was good for cleaning out the trombone, too, of course.

I'll bet it was! So tell me a little bit about your time in Stalagluft 3.

BILL: Well, I was shot down in the Mediterranean Sea in early '42 and I was a prisoner in Italy until the end of the Italian war, and then we were taken to Stalagluft 3 where we spent the rest of the war. It was just out of Germany, really, in Poland, and we existed there for the next year or two, so in total I was a prisoner for about three years. I'm one of the only survivors from the Great Escape so I've just been lucky right through, because I was shot down well out to sea and we swam in, pulling in one of our crewmen who was very badly burnt. So I was just very, very lucky.

Yeah, I'll say! And you tasted the fruits of the trombone, mate. I'll bet it was lovely.

BILL: Oh, it was marvellous.

I might try that with mine, because my playing's not coming along as well as it might do, Bill.

BILL: It probably needs cleaning out. In the camp we got Healthy Life lemon crystals in our Red Cross parcels so we used to boil this up and get the lemon flavouring off the gelatine—we used the gelatine to forge, or print, maps and things like that by an offset process—so that when you mixed the lemon flavouring

A 'Rough' Red

155

with the alcohol you got a most marvellous, lemon-flavoured drink which was so good you could get over the wire with it!

Look, Bill, I'm sure it wouldn't have tasted as good in a saxophone, for instance.

BILL: Oh, definitely not. The trombone was the secret.

Exactly! Bill, I'm disappointed you don't like my music much, but we'll keep playing trombone music for you. It was lovely to talk to you.

30 JANUARY 1994

Bill Fordyce rang up once before. He was a prisoner of war during the Second World War and he told us that the only good thing about trombones was that in the camp they used to use a trombone to distil the local jungle juice. We're in the Melbourne studios now, and guess who's turned up—Bill Fordyce—and he tells me that 25 March 1994 will be the fiftieth anniversary of the Great Escape. Bill was in that, so it's a great pleasure to talk to him. How old are you, Bill?

BILL: I'll be eighty on 30 March, just after the anniversary.

Tell me about the Great Escape and your part in it.

BILL: Well, firstly, there was virtually a lottery to decide who in the camp would be in the escape. The important people were numbers one to about forty and people who worked in various avenues on the escape were next, and I was lucky, I drew number eighty-four. I say I was lucky because earlier than that I might have been amongst the men shot, and later than that I wouldn't have been in the tunnel. However, I was in the tunnel—and perhaps I should tell you that it was thirty feet deep, 310 feet long, and twenty-four inches square, so it was very, very claustrophobic. I was just coming out of the exit—it was broad daylight by this time because all sorts of things had happened; there was an air raid which put the lights out—the tunnel was electrically lit; then the tunnel collapsed on several people and the diggers had to go in and dig them out—so by the time I got through it was daylight, and I was just about to come up at the exit when someone screamed out, 'Get back, the goons are here!' and there was a lot of firing. Then they started to shoot along the tunnel and, being the greatest coward in the world, I turned around and crawled back again.

PICNICS IN THE PARK

One of the many joys the program brings me is meeting people during our outside broadcasts. When the ABC holds its Picnics in the Park, it doesn't matter in which town or city, the time of day or the state of the weather, they come in their thousands. And I love it . . .

MORE FROM ULTIMO

More scenes from the Ultimo concert. Smoky Dawson, now over eighty but looking sixty, keeps on entertaining and the crowd loved his song. Here's a close-up of 'Digger' Revell, who was made very welcome. Regular listeners will know all about Peter Allen's maracas. The amazing thing is that despite the fact they've been handed around during countless concerts, no-one's bothered to pinch them - yet!

You could turn around?

BILL: Only just; it was very difficult, as you can imagine—twenty-four inches. The thing that decided the size of the tunnel was the fact that the bed boards that we slept on were twenty-four inches long and the tunnel was shored up with bed boards, and therefore it was twenty-four inches square. It had a little railway in it, and it was air-conditioned, of course—it needed to be, down there—and you lay on this little truck with your arms straight out in front of you and were towed along by the man in what we called the half-way house, further along.

Amazing! Tell me, Bill, was the escape on because conditions were bad, or because it was your duty to escape?

BILL: That was the reason. At the time there were three tunnels going, called Tom, Dick and Harry, and this was the biggest and the one that was just about to break.

What was it like in the camp? Was it pretty rough?

BILL: Well, I thought it was terribly rough, but when I spoke to people from prison camps in Japan I realised that we had an absolute picnic. It was very tough, though. If you did as you were told all the time, which nobody ever did, all that happened was you were very, very hungry. I came out weighing just about seven stone.

Despite the distilled essence of trombone! Did someone play it in the offtime?

BILL: We had a very good band, with instruments sent by the Red Cross. Looking back on it you forget all the hard parts and remember the extraordinarily funny parts. It was a good way of dieting, too!

What were the circumstances that led to you becoming a prisoner of war?

BILL: I was flying a torpedo Wellington over the Mediterranean Sea and we were shot down about ten miles offshore. The tail gunner was killed in the air and the rest of us were burnt and shot but we swam in, towing one man. We ended up in Benghazi and because I was an officer and the rest of the crew were sergeants I was flown to Italy. The other men were sent in a hospital ship, which was sunk by the Brits. So I was the only one to get away with it, really.

157

Are they having a reunion for the Great Escape?

BILL: They're having a commemorative service at London's St Clement Dane, the Air Force church, for the fifty men who were killed. Well, I've been trying to con a couple of airlines to give me free tickets, but unfortunately they won't—it's a lot of money these days. But I'm still trying—ever hopeful—and I've got the rather forceful Bruce Ruxton trying, and if he can't do it, nobody can!

Tell me about living in Melbourne.

BILL: I think it's a wonderful place. The weather's a bit hard to take at times.

You get all the seasons in one day here! You're looking pretty fit, Bill.

BILL: It's clean living—no grog, no sex, no women, no fun! It's in your genes, I think—I'm just lucky, I guess.

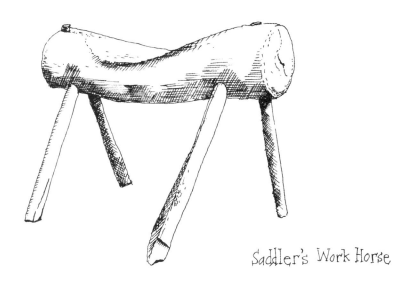

Saddler's Work Horse

TRAINS

I like the sight and sounds of old steam trains. Maybe they remind me of a time, not that long ago, when life was simpler, friendlier, more personal. Listeners will all know Gilbert Bennion. He's everyone's idea of a nice bloke and whenever he calls the program he entertains us just as Mary did. Gilbert's an old railway man, a gentleman, and he has a million railway stories. There's a great one which you'll find here in the interview I did with him.

When you spoke about the railways, and how they would continue if the politicians used them, I recalled some years back—1958. My home in Melbourne, my work in Queanbeyan, New South Wales, I would travel on the night train to Albury, then change over the platform to the New South Wales train. Added to that train was an extra carriage for a politician. I was told it was Arthur Calwell who didn't like flying. I never saw him, as I travelled second class, but I would be given a blanket for sleep. When the train reached Goulburn the carriage would be unhooked and then we would be hooked on to the train going south from Sydney to Canberra. When we were heading south the guard would come in with a cuppa for me, too. You can imagine it was a gentle way to travel and I would be ready for the afternoon shift at the hospital, refreshed and most grateful to that unseen politician.

From: Clare Pree, Broadmeadows, Victoria

I would like to share with you a recent experience I had while travelling through the New England and Hunter regions of New South Wales.

After a long morning's travel, I came by a most attractive little railway station at Scone. This station is operated by young, enterprising local ladies, not only as an efficient railway station—yes, the trains still frequent this station—but also as a flourishing retail outlet for local art, handcrafts and history, as well as operating a wonderful railway restaurant. (My daughter still claims her steak was the best she has had in her whole nineteen years, and that is some statement coming from someone who was born and bred on a cattle property in North Queensland!) As an adjunct to this operation these ladies frequently run cooking classes for all who are interested.

It leaves one with a warm feeling that at Scone private enterprise is helping to keep the trains operating and our history on the rails at the same time.

From: Merrelyn Cannon, Clayfield, Queensland

You broadcast and published in your first book my story about travelling to Deniliquin by train in 1940, how the train crew stopped everything while they walked to a nearby farmhouse to listen to the running of the Melbourne Cup!

That broadcast has had a most amazing consequence for me. The very next morning I received a phone call from a lady who turned out to be a cousin whom I had never met. She heard you give my name and the suburb where I live in Melbourne and so could trace me through the phone book. We are both in our seventies and this was the first time we had spoken to each other in all those years. And now three days after your program we have met and, among other things, discovered that we are descended from a marine who was on the flagship of the First Fleet, the *Sirius*.

I thought you may be interested in the historical reasons why we have our well-known problem of multiple gauge rail lines in Australia.

When railways were first considered in Australia the British Government decided that all the colonies should use the standard 4ft 8½in gauge. So far so good, and New South Wales, Victoria and South Australia started to plan railways.

Problems arose when the Irish engineer working for the railway company in Sydney convinced that company that the Irish broad gauge of 5ft 3in would be better. They proceeded with this decision, so Victoria and South Australia changed their plans and switched their equipment orders to 5ft 3in to fit with New South Wales.

This uniformity was disrupted when the Irish engineer resigned, or was pushed, and was replaced by a Scotsman, who was a firm believer in the standard 4ft 8½in gauge. New South Wales changed again and the other two States, who were notified late, refused to change again and lose money on equipment already ordered.

Thus was born our divided gauge. Where did the narrow Queensland, West Australian and narrow part of the South Australian system come from? Pure economics! With small populations and large distances they were forced into the cheapest option.

We are but a small fettling gang, four in all, operating out of Yaraka. Yaraka is a small community situated in the foothills of the Yang Yang Range and is the end of the section of track from Jericho. Our little community has thirty-one in all. We have an hotel, a store, a police station, a railway station and a school. Now it looks like it will become another victim to the three Rs—rationalisation, restructuring and regionalisation. This not only means the railway workers will be forced to relocate to some unknown destination or take redundancy, or even quit because there is no other option, but also the town may slowly disappear as other small communities have done with the disappearance of the railway.

With drastic transformation right across the board, affecting the transportation of wool, stock and commodities for the store, hotel, graziers and local people, regionalisation will be the destruction of all small towns in outback Queensland. One has to wonder if this is the method or the madness behind governments to try to control people by keeping them in a centralised region.

Regionalisation may seem like a good idea to governments but it is a tragedy to people who have grown up and lived in these small towns all of their lives. Everything is so quickly taken from them and there is no way around it, only to accept what has happened.

From: **Robert Long, Yaraka, Queensland**

When Sue of Quilpie was talking about the proposed closing of the rail line to Quilpie, I felt I must say something in support of what she said. I lived in Quilpie for twenty-eight years and spent over fifty years in that district.

Quilpie was always a great little place to get a job. At times some would leave for a year or so, but if they did not do well they could always come back to Quilpie. During the time of the Menzies Government a sealed road was built from Windorah to bring the cattle to the rail head and Quilpie was the biggest trucking centre in Australia. I have seen ten big stock trains leave there in two days. Now, to think that any government would dream of closing this line—well, it's unbelievable. Railway lines to the west are life lines and any governments that have ideas of closing them are sending the country backwards fast.

Note: Norman Macnamara's book *From Clancy's Day to Mine* tells the story of his pioneering family—his grandfather was 'Clancy of the Overflow'—and how he grew up and worked in Queensland.

From: **Norman Macnamara, Roma, Queensland**

I grew up in the twenties and thirties with my family at Taringa, a suburb on the Ipswich line. My father was what would be described now as a train fanatic. We all relied on him totally as a timetable. He knew the times of all the trains both going into and coming home from Brisbane—and if you were going to Ipswich he could tell you where it stopped on the way.

The most exciting times were when the mail trains were passing through. The two main 'mail' trains on our line were to Toowoomba and Wallangra. We lived about half a mile from Taringa station and from the back verandah had an excellent view of the trains as they passed by Taringa heading for Toowong or vice versa.

163

The warning would come from 'Dad's Den'—'three minutes to the Toowoomba *Mail*'. Most of us (there were nine children) would then start bolting the rest of our breakfast. Then as he heard the squeal of the wheels as the train negotiated a tight turn after passing through Toowong, Dad would bellow 'HERE IT COMES'. This created an immediate stampede as the enthusiastic mob hurled themselves out the kitchen door and up the stairs onto the back verandah armed with tea towels, aprons or anything to wave, the youngest ones screaming and crying if they didn't have a 'hanky'.

But the interest in the Toowoomba Mail was mild compared with that shown for the Wallangarra Mail. This train was one of Queensland's best, with beautiful heavy-style coaches, with a much more curved roof than the suburban ones. It was painted a dark red brown colour, and had 'ROYAL MAIL' printed in gold on the side as well as the royal insignia. The windows of the sleepers were frosted with white paint to stop people looking on the occupants. A train going to Wallangarra might just as well be going to the end of the earth as far as we were concerned. When Dad shouted from his den (he never came up himself) 'Wallangarra Mail— here she comes', all the rest of us, including Mum, stampeded to the back verandah from all over the house to gaze with awe as 'she' rocketed by in all her mysterious splendour.

On the rare occasions when Mother decided to take us all into the city the tension and energy expended in bathing (no hot water laid on) and dressing the four or five youngest ones was dreadful. Then as Mum struggled to dress herself and the train arrival time was approaching we would be despatched with many cautions for the walk to the station, with Mum racing down our street to catch us up.

We were lucky if the train drew into the station before we could quite make it because the road was right beside the railway line and Mum would wave her gloved hand and shout out to the driver, 'HOLD THE TRAIN, DRIVER'. The little scene that he looked down on—nine children streaming out and poor red-faced Mum trying to make it at the back—must have brought out the best in him because he always 'held the train' as we fought our way up the steep stairs across the overbridge and down into the train, helped by the Station Master (whose face was also red). Then Mum settled us all down like a hen with a clutch of chickens with a warning about not to lean out the window or we would get soot in our eyes. Someone always did, of course!

From: **Rona Wells, Tin Can Bay, Queensland**

IAN TALKS WITH GILBERT BENNION

One of the big thrills I had was when a bloke rang up from Tweed Heads. His name was Gilbert Bennion and he was 93. Well, ladies and gentlemen, he's now 94 and he's here today. How are you, Gilbert?

GILBERT: Pretty well—ready for anything that comes or goes!

Your birthday was 1st October. Happy birthday for your 94th.

GILBERT: Thank you.

When I first talked to Gilbert I said, 'Gilbert, how do you manage to keep going?', and he said, 'Well, I do my exercises—twenty minutes on the mat every morning'. I rang the other day and said to his wife, 'I'd really like Gilbert to come up and meet the people' and she said, 'Yes, I think that'd be all right, just check in a couple of days'. So I rang back and said, 'How's Gilbert going', and she said, 'Oh, he's all right. He just got out of the bath and he's doing his exercises in the nude!' I couldn't believe it!

But, anyway, Gilbert's here now and he can tell you a lot of stories. You worked with the railways for how long, Gilbert?

GILBERT: Fifty-one years, nine months, three weeks and one day! (laughter and applause)

That sounds like one of those jobs where you were counting every second till you finished.

GILBERT: Yes, that's right. In fact, they were short of staff at the time when I retired in 1964 and they said, 'You're an experienced man; we'll hold you for twelve months if you wish', so I stayed for an extra year.

Gilbert was also a great fisherman. I asked him what bait he used and he said 'Mullet-gut—the bream will leave home for that!' You also followed Smithy's flight, didn't you.

GILBERT: Yes, I did. I was keen on wireless and I built myself a two-valve wireless set. I put a wire up thirty feet in the air and after working on this set for quite a while do you know what I got? I got the Philippine Islands working with San

165

Francisco. I thought I was in the business world! But I did enjoy it; I followed Smith's flight from Fiji to Australia on the morse code and every hour he gave his latitude and longitude and Stan, the wireless operator, gave a few remarks, too. On one occasion he said, 'We're right above the clouds and it's very cold up here in the wee hours of the morning, and Smithy's promised us a nip of Scotch all round to get us ready for daybreak'. Another time he was just above the waves and I thought what a danger it was. Finally, when he arrived on the Australian coast he overshot Brisbane and came back. I was on duty that morning and just as he was landing in Brisbane a train came to the signals and I said, 'Bugger the trains!' (laughter)

Gilbert was a stickler for time and a great employee of the railways but you've got to remember that this one time when Smithy flew from England to Australia was a great event, so Gilbert said, 'Bugger the railways!'

GILBERT: So when Smithy landed I raced across and pulled the signals and brought the train in, and I said to the chaps, 'You know, I've been listening to history—Australia's wonderful history. Smithy's just landed'. They said, 'We'll square off for you, there's no delay here'. So they squared off for me, see.

That's a lovely story. Gilbert's done a lot of things. He was a stenographer. Was that early on?

GILBERT: Yes, I joined as an apprentice clerk and I went to the technical college two nights a week to learn shorthand. I was down in the operating room learning to be a telegraphist, too, on the other nights, so I never had a girlfriend until I was about nineteen years old. (laughter)

And the boss used to call you in for stenography?

GILBERT: When the general manager wanted to have a good swear he wouldn't take any of the three lady typists.

Tell me some of the stories about your time on the railways. You worked in many places over Queensland, didn't you?

GILBERT: Yes. One Toowoomba night it was very foggy and I had to cross trains there. I was at a station between Spring Bluff and Toowoomba and a down train came along. I waited for the guard to give me a light to show whether his van was clear of the main line and I got no light at all, so I thought, oh, this is bad, because I had a double header coming up from Spring Bluff and he was nearly ready to challenge my signals. So I thought, I can't let him in, I don't know what the position is down there, and I had to run down and leave the signals against the up train and what did I find? I found the guard fast asleep when he should have been giving me a red or green light! I shouted at him to wake him and raced back to bring the other train in, and there were four angry men on the two engines. They said, 'What the hell did you stop us there for?' But if I'd let them go they'd have crashed into that van and thrown it into the mouth of the tunnel and the guard with it, too. So it just shows you that the railway man's first rule is safety first and you can't take anything for granted. That's a lesson I learned from that. Can I tell you a funny story?

Yes, you can tell us a funny one.

GILBERT: Years ago there was a guard who had a case of eggs from the Egg Board in Townsville to deliver to Oorindi, a little siding up near Cloncurry. When the time came the guard forgot to tell the driver to stop, so he thought, I'd better not take this case on, I'd better deliver it. So he threw it out (laughter) and twelve dozen eggs crashed down and not one was whole. The station manager wrote and made a claim against the railway and the guard's reply was:

The General Manager,
Townsville

I was on guard on 34 up and had a case of eggs for Oorindi.
This case of eggs was in perfectly good order when it left my
hands.

'Why don't the trains that cross the Nullarbor stop now and again to let tourists have a look around at this real outback area of Australia?' Here is my story:
On 13 February 1952, I, with three other male companions, left Adelaide by train for a holiday in Perth. We changed trains at Port Pirie and boarded the Trans-Australian Railway as it was then called. They were just then introducing diesel engines to replace the steam engines that had hauled the train since 1917. We happened to be on one of those trains that was experimenting with setting a new timetable for the newly introduced diesels.

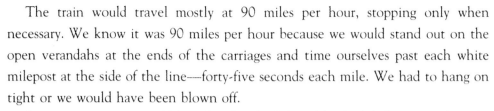

The train would travel mostly at 90 miles per hour, stopping only when necessary. We know it was 90 miles per hour because we would stand out on the open verandahs at the ends of the carriages and time ourselves past each white milepost at the side of the line—forty-five seconds each mile. We had to hang on tight or we would have been blown off.

So as not to arrive in Kalgoorlie ahead of the old scheduled time each night we would stop for three or four hours. We were told we could leave the train if we wished but to make sure we were back before departure time. Our first long stop was at Tarcoola at about 4.30 am. I had a friend in the Congregational Church ministry who was living there on his first appointment after graduating from college. At 6.00 am we decided to walk through to town and wake him up. It was easy to find the church and the house next door looked like the manse. We threw stones on the roof, called out his name and woke him up. He was naturally surprised but glad to see us and came back to the train and enjoyed a hearty breakfast.

Our next long stop was in the middle of the next night but I cannot pinpoint the name of the place. We thought we would go for a walk in the desert even though there was no moon. The conductor told us to keep the lights of the train in sight or we might never be seen again. We stumbled across a rough airfield with one plane and a tin shed. The wind indicator was hanging limp and it was extremely hot, even at that hour.

Our third and final long stop before Kalgoorlie was Rawlinna about 9.00 pm the next night. We were told we would be there till about 11.30 pm and that there was a dance in the local hall if we would like to attend. About half the trainload of passengers went to the dance including some of the train crew. Imagine the delight of the locals when all these people came into the hall from the train. The local fellas were extremely happy at the sight of the women who came from the train! Before our arrival there had been about thirty men and only five women at the dance. It was quite a night.

At 11.30 pm the whistle sounded and we were on our way again. It was a wonderful start to a wonderful holiday in the West and a great opportunity to meet and mix with the people who live and work on that great railway line.

From: **The Reverend Ian Russell, Wurtulla, Queensland**

A bit of interesting history was when they opened the railway from Mungar to Monto. One of the station masters sent a telegram to Brisbane to tell them that this station did not have a name and he would be obliged if they would send a name. So they spelt 'obliged' backwards and it ended up

DEGILBO. So that's what it is today, just up from Biggenden. All this was because the commissioner was coming up to run the line!

From: **Bill Law, Pialba, Queensland**

IAN TALKS WITH KEITH CRAIG

KEITH: I'm ringing about Paddy Hannan. In 1929, when I was twelve years old and went to North Kalgoorlie school, there was a competition to design Paddy Hannan's statue. Quite a lot of people went in for it and I won the competition.

Good on you! The statue is now in the main street of Kalgoorlie. And you were only twelve at the time.

KEITH: Only twelve. I'm seventy-five now and I'm swimming in the South Coast competition today in the Over-70s in the pool in Thirroul.

Mate, you'll freeze to death!

KEITH: It's very cold here this morning but we're used to it.

Tell us about going to school in North Kalgoorlie in 1929.

KEITH: In those days it was quite good fun. I lived in Ward Street and the trams used to run down by the school and it cost a penny to go that distance. We were pretty poor in those days and we used to run at the back of the tram and jump on and when the conductor came we'd go up the front of the tram and miss paying our fares. We were pretty smart when we were kids and we used to get up to all those tricks. Kalgoorlie was a great place in those days.

A good place to grow up in?

KEITH: Oh, yes, wonderful. The camaraderie there—the people were so good, everybody helped one another, it was fantastic. I was there when the riots were on, too. The miners were given a rough deal—they used to put on people who'd work for a small wage and our parents were unable to work. Riots started and a lot of people were killed. They burnt down hotels and shops—it was a terrifying thing at my age.

Kalgoorlie's still a bit of a frontier town. Tell me, you won the competition for the statue's design—what prize did you win?

KEITH: I won five guineas. They had a platform built at the time of the unveiling and I was presented with this five guineas—I thought I had a fortune! You could buy pies for threepence and drinks for a penny, and when I had five guineas I thought I was a millionaire.

A lot of money in those days, Keith.

KEITH: My word! I used to ride in the bike races—we rode from Menzies to Kalgoorlie. At the time there was Ozzie Nicholson, a Frenchman, and that great rider Oppy, and three of them rode against three of us on the Kalgoorlie Oval. They came over by train and they were pretty tired and we beat them! Ozzie patted me on the back and said, 'You'll be a great rider, son', and I never forgot that. I represented the State and we were to come over to Sydney to ride in the Velodrome. But the war broke out and I joined up and went overseas, so I didn't get the chance.

Isn't it funny the turns life takes, Keith? You might have ended up being one of Australia's greatest cyclists.

KEITH: Yes, I did love it. I've got my bike here now and I ride from Austinmer to Wollongong on the cycle track and I get a lot of enjoyment out of it.

Well, bike riding keeps you fit at seventy-five, eh?

KEITH: Oh, yes, and I could run. I ran in the City to Surf a few times but I don't do it now—I had a bit of a fall and it upset me a bit. But I'm going over to Kalgoorlie in September.

They have the Barrow Push in October, I think. Will you be over there for that? If we're over there too you look us up because I'd love to meet you, Keith. You haven't got any of that five guineas left, have you? We could go and buy a couple of pies!

WEATHER—SUNBURNT PLAINS AND FLOODING RAINS

The weather call on the program is hugely popular. Nancy Blake of Gunnedah in New South Wales wrote in defence of the weather call, 'It's the best weather coverage we get on radio all week. I know you must have time constraints trying to fit in all the stories, but the weather makes a pretty good (or bad) story, too. So I hope you don't cut down the coverage. Long live AAO!'

Nancy, the weather will stay! And this seems an appropriate place for a poem by Alan Binnie. Alan hails from Victoria so he should know!

WINTER IN MELBOURNE

The first sound of Winter is the dying echo
Of a ball that was cracked for a six
In the last innings of the season

The next sound of Winter is that of leather on leather
Of a goal being kicked from the half forward flank
Against a cold Southerly head-wind.

Kids seem to still play in the street
Terrorising the footpaths with their bikes
Or playing kick-to-kick in the court around the corner
Their noses and cheeks reddened
By cold air that bites
Despite the low brightness of a Winter sun.

Blokes breathe a sigh of relief
Knowing that the grass won't grow for a few months
And they tend to potter about in the shed
Sawdust on the workbench.

The kitchen windows steam up
Vegie soups boiling on the stove
And bread is cut into thick, crusty chunks.

The nights are longer and darker
And made for talking late
Maybe an old movie
And a hot cuppa to end the day.

Re *Send 'er down Hughie*. I first heard this expression about fifty-five years ago at the onset of a thunderstorm, and a bloke said, 'Send 'er down Juie' (or Jooey if you like). I asked him who was Juie, and his answer was 'Jupiter Pluvius, the god of rain'.

It has probably been changed to Hughie because it's a familiar name. My dictionary says that Jupiter was the supreme deity of the ancient Romans, the god of the heavens, whose weapon was the thunderbolt. I wouldn't know whether the Pluvius bit is authentic. Whatever his name, he's a temperamental bugger, isn't he?

From: Ian MacGregor, Bridgewater, Tasmania

Recently I came across this brief poem in a book written a hundred years ago in the US. The author was a shepherd in the Rocky Mountains in Idaho. With tens of thousands of drought-stricken sheep on the roads and stock routes of western Queensland I thought it appropriate to circumstances a hundred years later.

I've summered in the tropics,
Had the yellow fever chill,
I've wintered in the Arctic,
Known every ache and ill,
Been shanghaied on a whaler
And stranded in the deep
But I didn't know what misery was
Till I started droving sheep.

From: Colin Clift, Charleville, Queensland

I wish to lodge a formal protest about that 'Fog Pusher Bloke' on the bullbar near Esperance.

At dawn this morning in Albury the sky was crystal clear, not a wisp of fog on the horizon. Then I heard that 'Fog Pusher Bloke's Mate' talking about how thick the fog was.

I knew it would be trouble!

At 8.15 am EST that fog arrived in Albury. It was so thick that even the reverse-charge operator's voice (she was very polite) sounded foggy and she explained that the line to Sydney was fogged up so she couldn't make the connection to AAO.

That 'Fog Pusher' on the bullbar must have shoved the fog into the Roaring Forties. Hence its quick and unwelcome arrival in Albury. I'm not sure how far it is from Esperance to Albury 'as the fog flies'. It must be some sort of record!

'Fog Pusher Blokes' on bullbars should be banned in Esperance unless the 'Esperance Doctor' is blowing and then they would end up back in the cab with their mates where they ought to be anyway.

The fog's that thick in Albury this morning we can't see interstate, which is normally the case. I blame the 'Fog Pusher and his Mate' for it all!

PS It's 10.00 am EST and I had to stop writing because I couldn't see the paper to write even though every light in the house is on!

From: **John Josselyn, Albury, New South Wales**

NOW THE WEATHER

'And now for the weather,' came over the air,
We knew it was warm, so we just didn't care
'Expect *shattered scours*' then came from the gent,
We heard what he said and we knew what he meant

He said, 'In the morning there'll be a cool change,
And rain from the north is forecast for the range,
And thick *frogs and fosts* . . .' then his voice sort of went,
We heard what he said and we knew what he meant

'There'll be *wendy wither*, the front is depressed,
With some *snail and hoe* in the south and the west'
The longer he spoke just increased his torment,
We heard what he said and we knew what he meant

He finally screamed and let go with a sob,
As he said, 'I'm so sick of this *jorecasting fob*,
I'll just have to chuck it', so went his lament,
We heard what he said and we knew what he meant.

From: **Ron Strahan, Sofala, New South Wales**

We are in the middle of the worst drought in people's memories. These are desperate times and people on the land are going broke so quickly it's not funny. Desperate times result in people taking desperate measures to keep their cattle from starving.

I lock my cattle up every afternoon and feed them in the paddock. Each morning around nine I open the gate and let them out. I know some of them have been going out on the roadside where there is plenty of grass—some of it is even green! Most afternoons they are all back and locked up by three.

Today I had a visit from the pound-keeper. I am grateful he didn't get any of my cows which had been out. He says he'll be back and next time they won't get away. I realise he has a job to do and I accept his unenviable task in the current situation.

I feel that if councils and politicians were genuine about their sympathy and wish to help the man on the land, surely in times such as these the roadsides could be opened up and grazed, particularly in daylight hours. You just wouldn't believe how much feed is around and could be used at no cost to anyone.

The advantages would be obvious as councils would save on slashing. The edges would be clearer and drivers would be less likely to have kangaroos jumping out of the undergrowth in front of their cars. Most areas where this would apply are low traffic areas and signs could be erected warning motorists that cattle graze between particular daylight hours set by each shire.

There is always the risk of accidents with cattle about, but there is a greater risk of hitting wildlife. No one to my knowledge has suggested the kangaroos be barred from grazing along the road verges.

I honestly believe my idea could save a lot of people from desperation and all it would cost would be a little bit of inconvenience to a few motorists, most of whom I believe would rather that than see government hand-outs, resulting in higher taxes for everyone.

From: Larraine Russell, Moonmera, Queensland

Now winter is almost over I thought a poem about spring might be in order.

You read a description about life in Margaret's chilly kingdom and it reminded me so much of our problems when we lived in the north of Scotland near Inverness. Houses were in very short supply after the war and we considered ourselves lucky to find an empty forester's cottage perched high in the hills behind Nairn.

There was no electricity, running water or bathroom. The road for the last three miles was a dirt track, water was obtainable from a beautiful spring thirty-seven steps down the hillside, two buckets at a time, the nearest neighbour was about three miles away and we had two small children. To supplement the spring water we collected rainwater in a beer barrel. During one long, frosty period, when the temperature did not rise above freezing point, the surface of the water in the barrel froze and I had to knock a hole in the ice to get water. Next time I went to get water I found that ice had formed on the water beneath the hole. Each time I went to the barrel I found a new sheet of ice had formed below the latest hole. By the end of the week there was a couple of inches of water in the bottom of the barrel, a series of sheets of ice each a few inches above the next and each with a jagged hole in the centre!

One day I pegged some nappies on the line in a freezing wind and as I walked back I noticed that the first one I had hung out was stiff as a board. As I passed it the wind blew it against my face and cut my cheek open. My face was so cold that I did not know I'd been cut until the blood began to trickle down my face after I'd warmed up a little by the fire!

In winter it was necessary to keep a hammer and the shovel inside the porch in case it snowed and a path had to be cleared to the dunny. The hammer was needed by the first visitor for the day to break the ice that had formed overnight on the wooden seat. But the view across the valley was wonderful!

SPRINGTIME IN VICTORIA

It's spring! It's that season the housekeeper loathes,
'Cos Mum's flat out laundering four season's clothes;
As temperatures yo-yo the Celsius scale
And rain, sun and snow alternate with a gale;

The sun shows its force with some sizzling days
And crisps all the grass and the seedlings you raise
Up come the clouds and your ageing joints creak
And back go the blankets you threw off last week.

The morning is cold so you plan a hot meal
By the time it is ready the heat makes you reel;
If cold meat and salad is what you have planned
Be quite sure the weather will misunderstand

And send a chill wind and some fine sleety rain
Then Dad and the kids will all start to complain!
You really can't win with Victoria's spring ...
A capricious, erratic, undisciplined thing!

From: Dorothy Watt, Briagolong, Victoria

IAN TALKS WITH ELEANOR WATSON

ELEANOR: I rang to talk about the weather.

Right, tell us about the weather.

ELEANOR: You can imagine that being in the desert in May it's warm in the day with cooler evenings, but we've had some unseasonal weather. Last night we were driving from Halls Creek through to home after the school holidays; it was overcast and a thunderstorm set fires going right across the horizon. Can you imagine a vista of 360 degrees with beautiful fires burning on a totally black backdrop in the middle of an enormous desert? It was beautiful! Today it's overcast and very pungent smelling. The desert is the most beautiful place in the world.

It certainly is. It's a unique area. What are you doing out there, Eleanor? Why do we find you in the Great Sandy Desert?

ELEANOR: The Great Red Sandy Desert. I'm teaching here. I've been in the Kimberleys off and on for sixteen years and I head towards the city every so often and think, oh, back to civilisation, and then back I come. I just can't resist it. I've taught in areas like Halls Creek, Wyndham, Kununurra, but this year is the first time I've taught in a remote community and it's a unique experience, possibly because I'm with a unique community here. It's been a relatively sheltered community, the people still speak their own language—English is a second language—and they're working towards self-determination. It's a great experience. Certainly, one gets to understand the love of the land and why it's such a great commitment to retain it in their culture.

I don't think people appreciate just how beautiful the desert is. I think they've got a vision of the Gibson Desert and places like that.

A Day's Wear in Melbourne

177

Or the Sahara Desert—just sand. It's nothing like that, is it?

ELEANOR: No. The horrible thing is that I believe they've discovered a lot more gold at Halls Creek and that will be upgraded next year. My first teaching appointment was Halls Creek in about 1959 so I remember it as it used to be, not unlike where I am now. Now they're getting an international airport, I believe, so I'm just hoping they don't discover too much gold out here!

I must say I tend to agree with you. I'm looking at the map—where are you?

ELEANOR: Balgo Hills is about 300 miles south east of Halls Creek towards the Northern Territory. It used to be an old Catholic mission but it's now moving towards being a self-determining Aboriginal community. It's certainly remote. You go along the Tanami Desert and you turn off at a sign that says Balgo and go on about 50 kilometres. There's a 'Road Closed' sign, but you couldn't really call it a road; it's sort of a sandy pathway! So it's very isolated. They do have an aeroplane but it's only got one propeller—I don't like that, I like at least two propellers and mature men with grey hair driving it!

Everybody here is nodding in agreement, Eleanor! You're a woman after our own heart—two engines are better than one. So the weather's getting a bit colder.

ELEANOR: Two weeks ago we had the coldest overnight temperature in the State; it got down to eight degrees.

I wonder if you're getting more rain in the desert than in years gone by, Eleanor.

ELEANOR: Well, they say the average rainfall here is eight inches and last year I think they had thirty-seven. There's been massive flooding: there's a small creek here called Sturt Creek that comes down from the north, and it was nearly two kilometres across and up to fifteen feet deep in the centre. That cut us off from the middle of January to about three weeks ago. To get in you had to go around via Lake Gregory—which, incidentally, is another Lake Eyre. I believe it's six times the size of Sydney Harbour, although why everyone uses Sydney Harbour as a benchmark I don't know!

Engineers use it as a unit of measurement—they call it Syd Harbs—they say they're building a dam and it's six or ten or whatever Syd Harbs. But, Eleanor, what do you teach out there?

ELEANOR: English is a second language here and I take the secondary students and teach them life survival skills for later on, which are very different, as you can imagine, to their counterparts down south. It's called Luurnpa and that means 'the path of the kingfisher'. I'll never forget the first day that I saw the kingfishers come in here—I had the hose on and some hundreds of kingfishers turned against the sun and you saw the blues and the golds—a most beautiful sight. The budgies breed out here and they have very brilliant colours that you never see in caged birds. Cockatoos, topknot pigeons, spinifex pigeons, there's such prolific bird life. But possibly the main thing about Balgo is that evidently it's the centre of the Aboriginal art world, and I never cease to be amazed: some of the women out here who are still very tribalised have been all round the world. There are paintings from Balgo that hang in famous art galleries all over the world.

Eleanor, you're making us wish we were out at Balgo right now.

ELEANOR: It used to be a Catholic mission run by German missionaries and the *pièce de resistance* is the beautiful stone architecture. We have the most wonderful church here—you sit on top of the mesa and the mesa breaks away and you look across 360 degrees—it's a marvellous vista. It's very spiritual—probably because the Jesuits are planted here! What the German priests have done is mix and match the Aboriginal icons with the Catholic icons, and you have this wonderful mixture of two cultures which has actually worked. Our Easter celebrations went on for five days, and it was the most spiritual experience I've ever had, seeing the combination of true ritual Catholicism and Aboriginality, with their dancing and . . .

Isn't that lovely!

ELEANOR: It is; it's an atmosphere that you would never find anywhere else. I think it's an honour to be allowed to come out here; it's truly been a great experience.

Eleanor, we love talking to you. How come you rang us this morning—did you just sort of get the urge?

ELEANOR: Yes, when you were talking about the weather I thought there can be nothing more sensuous than smelling the dry earth after the first few drops of rain; the beautiful smells are wafted through from the greenery and I thought I'd love to share that with people because I know my own sons have a peculiar idea

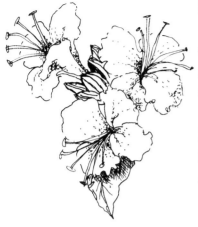

(See below.)

of what the desert is. What's that poem—'Many a flower is born to blush unseen and waste its fragrance on the desert air'—and I feel that that applies here because you can't communicate the beauty.

It applies to lots of Australia. That's the theory we run this program on—all the little blossoms that were born to bloom unseen flower here on Sunday mornings. And don't they flower—just like you, Eleanor!

At the suggestion of a Queensland friend I am sending you a poem I wrote in 1980 which seems to fit the situation today. (They are avid listeners up in Queensland.) By the way, her husband is terminally ill and your program comforts him a great deal. If perchance you read this poem on air could you please give mention to Joan and Len Catton of Bellmere, Queensland. I know the gesture would give great pleasure to my dearest friends. I have been writing Aussie poetry for many years (mainly bush verse) and was fortunate enough to win a Bicentennial prize with a poem entitled *The Scenic Highland Way*.

ABOUT DROUGHT

We were working in the garden when the doorbell rang that day
And my husband hurried in to open up
Then I heard a voice familiar, saying, 'Ow yer goin' Ray?
Put the kettle on an' get me favourite cup'

'Twas my mother's brother, Charlie, with his weatherbeaten face,
And a grin from ear to ear for both of us
'What's the matter with your writing hand?' I said with little grace
He heaved a sigh, and said 'Aw lass, don't fuss'

'Oh, I'm sorry Uncle Charlie. How you coping on the land?'
He turned to Ray and near choked on his drink;
Then as he wiped a sliding tear, he said, 'Please understand,
I'm fightin' drought, an Him upstairs I think

'I've been feedin' stock by hand, me boy, for nigh on eighteen months
But the feed I'm spreadin' now I'm spreadin' lean
The neighbours there can't help me, and the banks won't bear the brunt
So I guess I'll just keep prayin' fer the green

'I tell yer lad, it breaks me heart, ter see the cattle down
Them gazin' up at me through helpless eyes
And the blasted crows just waitin' ter set the table round
The stock I reared, which now I'm watchin' die

'Sure, this'll be the end of me, an' may I ask "Fer what?"
All those years of bloody yakka, gone ter waste
If I lost it all termorrer lad, I couldn't give a jot—
Let the devil have the Gawd-forsaken place

'Oh, I shouldn't be so harsh, I s'pose, I take the latter back
I guess it wasn't Christian, was it son?
I've just gotta stop this nonsense, an' let me mem'ry track
All the good years when me beef was number one'

Well, the conversation drifted to our kids and other things
And Ray took Uncle Charlie to the train—
And I wished I had a fortune for relief that money brings
But instead—I begged the Lord for soaking rain

From: Heather Prentice, Hawks Nest, New South Wales

How would you like to wake in the morning to find your false teeth frozen in their overnight resting place, a mug of water? This is a commonly-told tale in this area.

I was down by a shed water butt the other midday and the ice was at least one inch thick. And have you watched poor birds trying to have a bath in the bird bath which has been in the lukewarm sun for hours but is still frozen?

How about after a minus six degrees frost you pull back the curtains to find fine ice *inside* the window? You then have to go outside into the wind which is achingly cold. Sago snow, snow in minute flakes and snow in big flakes drift into the silence of a world huddled against the cold. Then, when the wind gets up, the snow slaps against the tree trunks. The snow is driven horizontally—there is no escape—put your head down and it goes down your back, look up and it goes all over your face and glasses and down your neck.

When first married we had thirty-two volt electricity until the 240-volt eventually came through. No electric blankets; we had satin-bound blankets and they would be like ice. I used to buy two sets of flannelette sheets so I could cut one in half and sew it to the bottom of the top sheet. This gave that extra length to turn back over the satin and to allow us to wrap the sheet around so no fingers of icy air penetrated down any minute gap.

Then came the 240-volt and electric blankets—oh, the praise heaped on the head of the unknown inventor! All bedrooms had heaters installed. The toilet—a heater, the bathroom—a heater, everywhere heaters—even the woolshed had fan heaters.

We have lost thousands of trees through frost and my husband, never daunted, keeps on planting and the trees grow during the summer—but come an early frost and nothing is left. Forestry extension officers have planned the plantings but no one's expertise is above the destruction of frosts.

The cold looks good if you are sitting beside one of those big windows at the Hydro Majestic with a good hot meal and the fires warming the place. But not when you have to live with it day and night for months on end!

From: Margaret Blaxland, Walcha, New South Wales

On two recent Sundays I have heard reference made to this year's excellent display of wild flowers in the Murchison, Gascoyne and Pilbara regions of Western Australia. My wife and I lived in the northern part of this state for a period of ten years, up to 1988. We have also returned there each year to enjoy some winter sunshine and good fishing. This year we headed north in April and already there were signs of relief from the drought which had plagued parts of the area for three years. In optimism I penned a little poem as the rain tumbled down.

RAINDROPS ON THE ROOF

I love the sound of raindrops
On the aluminium roof
Yes, I love to hear those raindrops
As they bring again the proof
That though this land be parched and dry

And people wonder when
This wondrous answer from the sky
Will fall and succour them
They wait for months with lead-filled hearts
As sheep and cattle die
They wonder why they stick it out
And battle not to cry
They see the tourists passing through
Enjoying endless sun
That spreads across this big red land
of rivers yet to run

But now the scene is changing
Green shoots transform the red
The cattle now will fatten
Wildflowers will grow and spread
From horizon to horizon
The birds will mate and sing
There'll be reason for rejoicing
And we'll know the very thing
That brought about this wondrous change
That gave us such great proof
Was the sounds I listen to tonight
Of raindrops on the roof

From: **L A Davis, Pinjarra, Western Australia**

AUTUMN

The Autumn winds are blowin'
On the ranges it's a'snowin'
All the stockmen are a'goin'
'Cause the Autumn winds are blowin'

To the city they are goin'
And their Holdens are a'slowin'
Because here it's bloody snowin'
In the city they'll be glowin'

Through the valleys and the ranges,
It hasn't been this cold for ages,
All doors are shut like cages,
As the fire glows and rages

Winter's opening like a blossom,
Sending every frog and possum,
To their homes by the crossin'
Away from winter's chilly frostin'

Outa work with me 'orse and dray,
Idlin' and doin' nothin' all day,
Far-off skies are stormy grey,
Another winter on the way

From: Bob Wilson, Mareeba, Queensland

IAN TALKS WITH GRAHAM MIDDLETON

I'm always amazed at what Australians get up to. I remember Keith Oliver who walked Australia from north to south following in the footsteps of George Ernest Morrison (Morrison of Peking). He rang us from time to time from different places as do many Australians who are walking/cycling/riding Australia.

But I think the journey that I was really in awe of was Graham Middleton's epic Murray River swim from the freezing head waters in the Snowy Mountains to the Coorong in South Australia, a journey of 2600 kilometres encompassing fifteen locks and weirs.

Graham rang us from time to time in his swim as he raised money for Kids in Cancer and you could tell in his voice as the weeks and months went by (it took 138 days) that the swim was taking its toll, mentally and physically. He spoke to me some weeks after he'd finished the swim.

G'day Graham—how's it going?

GRAHAM: We finished last week. On Wednesday, for the final swim, we went to the mouth of the Murray into Lake Alexandrina. I'm sorry I couldn't ring a couple of weeks ago but it was so mind-boggling that I couldn't concentrate and my time was so critical that I had to keep on going.

Was it as hard as you thought it would be?

GRAHAM: Yes, it was harder than one might have thought it was going to be, but it's been done now. I guess the biggest part was that it was the mind that had to be activated at the end, more than my body. The cold water and cold wind were really getting at me a bit, but it's been done and I thought I'd let you know.

The hardest thing you've probably ever done.

GRAHAM: Yes, totally the hardest thing I've ever done, for sure.

When you say 'swimming the Murray River' you just think, oh well, it's swimming the Murray River, and you take your time; but it's having to get up every morning and hop into the drink again, especially when it's cold like the Murray. Tell me what sort of things used to go through your mind.

GRAHAM: I guess we were always hoping we'd get a great result for our Kids in Cancer and especially in the later stages that kept on being very much part of my mind—to make certain that the challenge was also a very charitable event. But when it really got hard I'd have to exclude everything from my mind except what I was doing. In the mid part of the river I had plenty of time to contemplate and philosophise, but in the end it was absolutely a battle to keep my mind on the job and keep going. But anyway, we've done that. It took 138 days and I did it in consecutive days and it meant I was swimming in the water just on six hours, every day, for 138 days. Over four-and-a-half months. At the end we were watching the leaves go yellow for autumn and we started in the spring.

One hundred and thirty-eight days and six hours a day. Everybody here's just going 'ooh, aah'. So where are you ringing from now?

GRAHAM: I'm in Melbourne now. One day when I spoke to you I was really, really tired. That was when I was in Deniliquin, but I'm pretty good now. I'd say I'm back to about 90%, I'm driving my car and I'm with my family which is beaut. I'm about to go swimming again when I've finished this phone call.

You probably never want to see the Murray River again.

185

GRAHAM: I loved it, actually. I really did love it. We talked about pelicans the last time I spoke to you and there are so many beautiful things on the Murray. I guess as much as anything it was the people on the Murray who were fantastic—great people, full of encouragement and generosity. The water isn't that bad—I think I mentioned that the water's healthy when it's dirty and not when it's clean.

Isn't it funny that in the middle of summer the water's cold.

GRAHAM: Yes; it was ten degrees in December, that's Carlton United drinking water temperature.

I saw you on TV and you looked a bit tired.

GRAHAM: I guess I eventually had to get tired. But actually I think the river might have been kind to me and let me hang in, because it was very hard at the end. If I'd had really bad weather against me it might have been hard to finish, but the last few days the weather was good and the wind wasn't against me and the waves weren't coming at me. I guess the river fought me all the way and in the end let me through. I feel a bit humble about it actually.

WHY I LIVE WHERE I LIVE

The letters to 'Why I Live Where I Live' will make an excellent book. I suppose it's because they go to the soul of our being. Why do some stay where they are all their lives? Why do others change homes every few years? Others sell up and move interstate and some simply sell up and go on the road. As it says in the poem on page 194:

Macca I tell you, why I live where I live,
But on Sundays . . . I live where I like.

Not many people can say that they find comfort in having their hands in the warmth of the kitchen sink. I can!

When my family of six moved into this house many years ago, we had a dishwasher. It was in need of some minor repairs and the family just couldn't understand why I donated it to a charity for some industrious person to get it going again.

Mainly it's the view. The house is built against a hill. It's similar to the view from a treehouse, not unlike the one my son and his grandfather built in the tree to my left. The treehouse has deteriorated over the years but not before my son and his mates spent many hours 'restyling' it, their hammering and chatter echoing through the hills. We went through buckets of nails. 'A cheap toy', their father said, considering the cost of anti-social and expensive computer games.

The turning circle at the top of our drive is just below the window. It's here they learnt to ride their bikes (oh, my aching back!), skate, skateboard, skip, hopscotch and do the greatest 'slam dunks' into the basketball hoop my husband built above the carport entrance. It's here I can see their cars; that they're now home safely after being out late at night. It's here I can see the welcome arrival of friends or save the postman a long walk up with a heavy delivery.

There's a swing under the trees made from an old tyre and hung by a rope. Many a time I've watched my youngest daughter stand in it and swing high into the trees or lie back so that her long curls sweep the dry gum leaves on the ground.

I can watch down the valley for inclement weather coming and run out to 'save' the washing. The valleys meet with a triangle of ocean in the distance. When evening comes and the sun sinks into that ocean, it throws up a red glow to silhouette the gumtrees.

As I watch my ten-year-old son whirling round and round on his BMX, his hair standing on end and a grin of delight on his dirty face, I plunge another plate in the sink and count my blessings.

From: **Trudy Williams, Belair, South Australia**

Here I am on this beautiful Sunday morn, and I don't even have to leave my bed to see the ships waiting to berth, the boats scudding to and fro looking for good fishing spots, and the little yachts practising for the big race on New Year's Day.

I just love my little van where I can relax (I'm at the jetty caravan park at Wallaroo at the moment). Lately I've not been too well. I lost two very dear friends in tragic circumstances, so I needed the peace and beauty of this dear old town. It has a wealth of history. I care very much for the people who own the park—wonderful Australians! Jeanette is like a daughter to me. We were both laughing and crying over your program this morning. I had the radio on loud enough for her to hear while she was cleaning. I said to her that these days listening to *Australia All Over* is like going to church! It's uplifting, and makes me feel grateful for being alive, and humbled—all the tragic things happening around us are not so hard to bear. I don't mean to sound sacrilegious! Somehow it does give me a sense of peace, and gives some meaning to life that I find hard to match.

Going for my morning walks also does me a lot of good, spiritually and physically. I guess people are used to seeing me walking about in my red dressing gown, chatting to the local fishermen. Each story they tell me is more unreal than the last! It's a good way to start the day, with the smell of the sea in one's lungs, the air crystal clear and invigorating.

From: Zita Carew, Wynn Vale, South Australia

I am an Anglican priest. I have left the regular parish ministry in order to live in the Bulloo shire, which covers the seventy-three thousand square kilometres (twenty-eight thousand square miles) of south-west Queensland in the corner.

I came with one change of clothes, no money, no car and no house—just as the Bible says clergymen should. We do not take up a collection or charge for any Church services: 'Freely have you received, so freely give'. And I discourage donations, preferring paid work—honest labour.

I have never been so content, so fulfilled, so rich or so free. There must be dozens of places like this around the interior of Australia that have never had a resident minister of any church. And they are just waiting to make other clergy as content as I am.

PS   Would you believe I see every family in this vast area each couple of months. I go with the police, and with the mail trucks. And my Church notes go out to every family with the school newsletter. This must be the only Parish run on ZERO dollars, just for the love of it!

From: Keith Stevenson, Thargomindah, Queensland

As undoubtedly you have noticed, I have a foreign name. Yes, many moons ago we left our country of birth, Holland, to build a new future here in Australia. We came here in '53—all five of us, three children, the eldest not yet five, and another one on the way. We paid our own fares. We had a small farm in Holland which we, of course, had to sell. With the proceeds we paid our fares to this wonderful country.

We had English lessons for about half a year, twice a week for two hours. So if the people spoke slowly and clearly we could get a fair idea of what was said. Of course we made blunders in the beginning but we must give the Aussies credit, they never laughed at us in our face. They might have laughed later on after we had gone. Good luck to them—that did not hurt us.

In general we found the Aussies easy to get on with, if one was willing to adapt. The Aussies certainly did not push us back. On the contrary we found them helpful, friendly and genuine. Of course, like all beginnings we had difficult times but never have we been homesick. We had made the decision to build a better future for our children and stuck to it. Gladly, we can say we won.

We went back to Holland for the first time in '82 after twenty-nine years in Australia. We wanted to see what our relatives were up to. We were asked if we would settle back in Holland. No way! Give us this country any day—this glorious climate and these genuine people.

From: Herman Vandervget, Mullumbimby, New South Wales

Up here in the Gulf Country of the Northern Territory the ABC is our lifeline to the world, and your program brings the rest of this wonderful country right to us ordinary Aussies from 'All Over', gives us in isolation the reassurance we often need.

As I write this I am listening to your wonderful 'Bird Music'—to which in addition I have the supreme pleasure of hearing and seeing the real live ones joining in. As our home is 'open living'—louvres and verandahs best suited to a tropical climate—not only can we hear you in the workshop or garden, so can our multitude of feathered friends who join in joyously or with alarm at the sometimes 'strange' birds invading their realm. Our radio is via a 100w Codan—on relay from Darwin and Katherine, which also includes the Royal Flying Doctor frequency, used when necessary.

I don't need an alarm clock. I sleep out on the verandah now that the weather is warming up. My early morning call is the melodious trill of a bird in the shrubbery about three feet from my bed, just outside the screens. What a wonderful awakening (why hasn't someone invented an alarm clock that 'trills'?). To be so blessed, to have the privilege of listening to the various calls (I counted twelve different species of sounds this morning), to watch the daylight emerge, the horses come in for water, the stirring of the life that surrounds me, I must be the luckiest lady alive.

But I write this with sadness also. This will be the last program I will enjoy from the bush. Like many other 'Aussies from All Over' I am leaving the bush, the life I've always known, lived and loved; broken dreams, broken promises and finally broken heart. There are so many of us leaving the land these days, yet I hear that some Australians go hungry.

Ten years ago we came to this remote area of Australia. So much has been achieved, so much has been lost, good times and hard times, pioneers in a modern age—unbelievable but true. Bless you, Macca, for what you have done and are doing every Sunday morning for us ordinary Aussies.

From: Heather Galvin, Gulf Country, Northern Territory

I live in Charleville, a lovely town in south west Queensland, but the joy of my life is to take a trip out to Adavale, a tiny, almost deserted little township some two-hundred-odd kilometres from Charleville. My son and daughter-in-law own the little store and bottle licence there. Truly, Macca, you have to journey far outback to appreciate the true Australian and Australiana. Of course, the pub verandah is the 'in' place every night and yarns and deeds spoken of would make Mike Tyson look like a 'wimp'. Needless to say, the number of stubbies consumed seems to affect the size, numbers and magnificence of things discussed.

On one such night the conversation turned to fishing (Adavale, by the way, is situated on Blackwater Creek—a terrific fishing spot!) and truly, the number and size of the fish caught that night would have fed the population of Sydney for at least a decade. And the SIZE! You'd have to use a butcher's hook to land some of them. At one stage, I was very fortunate to escape with my life when one of my fishing mates and I almost capsized the boat hauling in an 85lb cod! Would you believe me if I told you it took me two and a half hours next morning to sweep the scales and fish gut off the verandah?

Next night the conversation turned to horses and horsemen and before you could get down from the saddle it got to rodeos and bull-dogging. Boy! Those boys are tough! And the dreadful injuries inflicted that night and medals won would make you proud to be an Aussie ringer. Next morning, though, proved quite profitable, as by the time I swept up and bagged the horse dung that was left lying on the verandah, I'd raised $50 for the Royal Flying Doctor by selling it to enthusiastic gardeners!

Some of the tales and yarns really should be recorded for posterity, as they contain the pure essence and philosophy of the Aussie bushman, and though times were incredibly tough, the humour seemed to shine through, and the toughest situation became a laugh. Funnily, all the stories you hear are TRUE—such as this one I was told by an old Adavale-ite.

Apparently, there was an Adavale chap who drove the Cobb & Co coach between Adavale and the next coach 'station' twice a week, and for years the lady at the change station always cooked him a meal of curry and rice (his favourite dish). On this one occasion he had a young English lass on board travelling to a job as governess on some outback station. She was very intrigued by her surroundings, this being her first experience in the bush, and was amazed to see a great grey kangaroo sitting placidly by the side of the road, quite close to the coach. The driver, having a joke at her expense, yelled to the 'roo, 'Hey mate, hop off down the road and tell Mrs Jones I'm on my way, and to have curry and rice ready for my dinner'.

Naturally the 'roo took fright and bounded off into the bush. Imagine the girl's surprise when they arrived at the coach stop to find a large plate of curry and rice waiting for them! She couldn't understand the intelligence of the great Aussie 'roo!

From: Joan Everitt, Charlevtlle, Queenaland

My Mum's name is Linda Barnes and she lives in a War Widow's unit in Sydney's Western Suburbs. Mum is a country person who must live in the city only for financial reasons and, although she makes the effort to get out and about every day, it is soul-destroying not to be able to hear a bird, or see the stars or a tree from her unit.

The units are situated in a shopping centre, opposite a railway station, so, with no neighbours, weekends and evenings are spent in fear of vandals. The rules and regulations the ladies must live by are so strict we now call the place 'The Cloisters'.

In the face of this, Mum has a wonderful sense of humour and is an avid explorer of the city and the bush, always hoping for the day when some miracle will occur to allow her to escape back to the country permanently.

We both enjoy *Australia All Over* immensely, but to Mum it is a soul reviver. Hearing all the lovely descriptions of where some people live often brings tears to her eyes. 'I dream of the day when I can write to Macca and tell him why I love to live where I live.'

Well, this is the best I can do to make at least part of a dream come true for her. She's a lovely lady, Macca, and I can assure you it would be a truly wonderful surprise for her to hear her name on Why I Live Where I Live.

WHY I LIVE WHERE I LIVE

I live where I live because I am trapped
Like a bird with no wings only vision,
Here at 'The Cloisters' we call this our home,
But really it's more like a prison

Lost in the suburbs where souls live in fear,
Locked behind doors in the city,
A bus ride away from the end of the day,
Where the scen'ry consists of graffiti

I live where I live but for no other reason,
A head must have somewhere to lay
But come Sunday morning I open my eyes
To AUSTRALIA ALL OVER . . . g'day

Now I can smell shearing sheds, gum trees and poddy calves
All at the flick of a dial
I can hear currawongs sing in the morning
I'm back in the bush for a while

Neilrex and Binalong, Bellbird and Billabong
Words you don't hear every day
I lived at Binnaway, then at Weetaliba
Years seem to just slip away

Lost in my memories I see in front of me
Mobs of red sheep in a drought
Then all of a sudden, I'm listening and knowing
What young Glen from Straddie's about

Housewives and pioneers enter my living room
Steam trains . . . trombone conventions!
Pussyplat? Platapi? laugh till I almost cry
Even lost dogs get a mention

Camp fires glowing, train whistle blowing . . .
A magical sound in the night
Macca I tell you, I live where I live,
But on Sundays . . . I live where I like

From: Lisa Kennedy, Marsden, Queensland

Until quite recently my husband and I used to listen to 'Macca' down in the milking shed but now, having sold up and moved into town, the surroundings are a little different and we can listen even more intently with fewer distractions. I think even Daisy and Co used to enjoy Sunday morning with Macca!

I have jotted down a few lines about Why I Live Where I Live in an attempt to reflect my feelings about rural living. I have lived in other country areas, although I was Melbourne born and bred, and also lived in suburban Sydney for seven years. I have found there is a strong sense of community and belonging in country towns and, although acceptance may take a while, once achieved it is a 'forever feeling'. City life lacks a sense of belonging and permanence for me.

From: Iris Barton, Numurkah, Victoria

My home is a bush timber and iron 'shack', situated twelve miles inside the Simpson Desert, with no-one for miles and miles north, south or east. To the west, there are two station homesteads within sixty miles. We nestle in a valley, flanked by two long red sand dunes, the colours of which change lots with the differing times of day. The valley is a watershed for a huge expanse of country to the north and north-east, so we can have water on three sides of us ('us' being the house and me), but that, of course, does not happen very often.

I love my spot because it is mine and because of the challenges it gives me every day. The moods of the desert are many and changes come quickly. I love to garden, but that is a real task and shakes my faith often, so any success is very sweet. I have succeeded with quite a few trees, so now have many birds. Different from when I first came here in 1955—three trees and glaring red sand then, with birds other than crows, hawks and galahs a real excitement.

I enjoy a little interaction with people. There are more and more folk coming through since the roads are improving greatly and it keeps me quite busy.

My only fear is that I may have to leave it before many more years. It gets a greater burden each year and it seems impossible to find anyone to share it with you.

I have rambled on, so enough. All the very best, Macca, and hang in there, because it is one of the only, if not *the* only, real thing we have left. One would think we should be ashamed of being Australians and our history. Fools! Long may *the* flag wave over us.

From: Molly Clark, Alice Springs, Northern Territory

The following five letters came from Class 6L of Our Lady of Lourdes School in Devonport, Tasmania.

I live where I live because our family wanted to move from New South Wales to Tasmania to buy a hotel motel.

I was born in Sydney, New South Wales. Our family lived in Wollongong for nine years, then moved to the Snowy Mountains for about a year and a half. Then after we left the Snowy Mountains we toured around Australia for about four months. After we had been around Australia we went to Tasmania where we decided to live.

We own a hotel motel called the Edgewater Hotel Motel in East Devonport. I have a brother and a sister whose names are Aimee and Adam. Aimee is in Year 5 and Adam is in prep. Aimee was born in Sydney and Adam was born in Wollongong. We like it where we live because it is on the water's edge and is near shops. I like living where I live.

From: Elise Kidd, East Devonport, Tasmania

My family moved to Devonport from Queensland because my Dad took redundancy from Mt Lyell, but mainly because we had always loved the coast. I live in a three-bedroom brick house in a quiet area in West Devonport. I like where I live because I have a friend over my back fence and another friend a short bike ride away. We don't own any pets, but I wish we had a dog. I like having the beach a short distance away because Queenstown didn't have one.

I have six people in my family. I live with my Mum and Dad and my seventeen-year-old brother. My sister is a teacher in Melbourne and is also married. My other brother, Andrew, lives in Hobart and is doing his last year of University. I miss them both a lot.

I have been learning the organ for two years, which I enjoy. My friends think

I can play well, but I don't really. I like Devonport's climate, but we have had a terrible winter. I can't wait till the summer and the pool opens. I play netball. My favourite position is goal attack. I also do gymnastics on Fridays. I've only been doing it for five weeks and I really like it. We have just learnt a new routine. *Well*, that just about covers everything about me, and that's why I live where I live.

From: Belinda Stevens, Devonport, Tasmania

I live where I live because we wanted a better opportunity in life. I originally came from Czechoslovakia where there is nothing for you to do in the future. Our house was really nice, I suppose. We had a cat and a few chickens. Here we have a cat, a dog and a budgerigar. We have a medium sized garden.

Every day after school Sarah Crabtree comes to our house and we go outside. We go down to the Fourways Shopping Complex because we live only two blocks from it.

Our neighbour is my Dad's best friend, so he goes to his house every weekend so we don't get to see him much. My Dad works in the Que River Mine and he only comes home on weekends.

Next year we may be moving to Brisbane, but I don't want to move. In Czechoslovakia we had much the same things as we have here, only we didn't have so much freedom. We lived straight in front of a forest, where we always played. The school was much further from our house than it is here. We had to walk to school in snow and hail.

My Mum had a lot on her mind. She worked in a kindergarten, where I went after school. I suppose I prefer living here. I miss my old home but I think my parents did what is best for us, and that is why I live where I live.

From: Petra Novak, Devonport, Tasmania

I live in McBride Street, Devonport, with my Dad and my sister in the government house. I like my house. It has a big garden behind the house. The house where I live is so nice and very cheap to rent. In my house is a beautiful cat. I like my cat too. My Dad likes to do the garden. He digs the garden every week and he grows some vegetables. We love the garden and we like living in Devonport. First I live in Vietnam with my Mum and Dad and my four sisters. I feel happy. When I went to Thailand I live in a camp and I feel lonely and homesick. I lived with my Dad and my sister in a little house. In Thailand it is not free for everybody in the camp. After that we went to Australia and we feel very happy and we like living in Devonport. I have a big house and a huge garden and we enjoy living in the house and garden and very good for I go to school.

From: Ngoc Huynh, Devonport, Tasmania

I like living where I live because it's quiet and peaceful. My parents and family like living in Devonport because everyone is friendly. We own six acres and raise lots of animals.

They are—2 dogs, 2 budgies, 2 horses, 2 ducks, 2 canaries, 1 cat, 1 goat and lots of ducklings.

We live on a hill in Spreyton—a lovely spot. We are still part of Braddon (Devonport). When I go to bed I feel safe. When I ride my horse around, I enjoy seeing the fresh green paddocks. We live inland and it hardly ever floods.

I live on the north west coast of Tasmania. I live with both my parents. I have lots of friends living near me. My parents originally come from Chile and say that Tasmania is so different from Chile.

From: Cardine Cossio, Spreyton, Tasmania

Gunnedah has everything I want and need—a rich farming district, where they grow wheat, cotton, grain sorghum, sunflowers, cattle, sheep and wool, pigs and even a snail farm. Also a good climate.

Dorothea MacKellar, the noted poet, spent her younger days here and I believe it was after a long drought in Gunnedah had broken that she was inspired to write her famous poem *My Country.* We have a memorial to her in Anzac Park. Dorothea is seated side-saddle on a life-size horse which is drinking from a waterhole. The statue is cast in bronze. She used to live on the property 'Kurrumbede'.

We have a Big Tomato contest each January to see who can grow the biggest tomato and other novelty growing events with beaut trophies, music, talent quest— a big Carnival day.

We also have a big three-day event, Ag-Quip. It's a great exhibition of giant farming and country equipment which attracts thousands of visitors, quite a lot of exhibitors from overseas and the accommodation is booked out for miles around. This is the biggest field day in Australia and in the middle of the week we have a big Mardi Gras at night with the Australian Billy Boiling Contest, always a lot of fun, which they run at the Railway Hotel.

From: Len Peasley, Gunnedah, New South Wales

We live in a lovely warm solar electric house perched above the banks of the Bombala River, between Nimmitabel and Bombala. We look onto a natural trout pond, with babbling brooks burbling down and making lovely sounds running smoothly over the rocks; we have built a patio out the front of our kitchen glass doors and, looking at the river this morning at minus six degrees and frosty, raining, misty and the birds grateful for their morning repast, I feel happy and contented and lovely and warm with our combustion stove and loungeroom stove going, kettle always on the boil.

A wombat has just ambled down past our lawn—probably had a feed of my baby lettuce! Dolly our border collie is romping around in the frost after spending the night luxuriating in front of the fire with a rug roughed up like a nest. Good life, eh?

I spin, paint, pot and generally irritate my dear 'Old Fella'. Barry is a chronic asthmatic who is very happy in this climate, the air is so pure.

As I am writing it has just started to snow gently—we will be tucked in for the day—BLISS!

From: Betty Braden, Nimmitabel, New South Wales

I live at Goode Beach, Albany, Western Australia.

Albany is located on the southern coast south, south-east of Perth. To me, Albany is just about the most beautiful place in the world; it encompasses three very fine natural harbours, Princess Royal Harbour, Outer Harbour and magnificent King George Sound.

From dozens and dozens of locations around Albany the scenery is different and spectacular. The whole area is also known as the Rainbow Coast and rainbows add another dimension to an already spectacular coast. I have actually stood only a few metres from the base of a rainbow as it moved from the land out into the Sound. It was breathtaking.

The climate here is near perfect, although some would disagree with me and say it is perfect. There are many retired people in and around Albany and I think this indicates that we are as near to bliss and relaxation as one can get. In season the wildflowers are on their own—they are unique and tourists come from everywhere to see them. We even have kangaroos and rabbits helping to keep our lawn trimmed. For those reasons and many more my wife and I chose to live here. We sometimes remark to each other 'There must be someone looking after us, for us to be so lucky to be here'.

From: Michael Mettam, Albany, Weatern Australia

SUNDAY MORNING

I must talk about Sunday morning
Here in Sydney's conglomerate sprawl
Balmain is the suburb
I live in with my all

The peace and quiet is noisy
From birds out in the yard
I'm listening to 'Macca'
Yes—life sure is hard

My dogs are resting
Nipping the occasional flea
Yes—you'd think you were in the country
Out where I'd want to be

No noise—it's so deafening
People are all at rest
Mowers are cold and tucked away
That way, it's just the best

Tomorrow is Monday
Back to noisy sound
Cars, planes and traffic
Will be back, you'll be bound

From: Frank Cashman, Balmain, New South Wales

My little bit of Heaven is Victor Harbor, a beautiful holiday resort on the Fleurieu Peninsula about fifty miles south of Adelaide. Our home overlooks the harbor, where we can watch the southern right whales as they frolic in the bay, also watch the glorious sight of the 'One and All' sailing vessel in full sail contrasted against the blue sky when it visits the area.

We can see the horse-drawn trams crossing the causeway taking happy holiday makers on a trip to Granite Island. A horse-drawn tram service operated between 1895 and 1954 when it was discontinued, but in 1986 re-created trams brought the past to life again. It is the only horse-drawn tramway in Australia.

Then at weekends we watch with delight as the majestic 520 class steam locomotive arrives in Victor Harbor hauling the 'Steam Ranger' day excursions from Adelaide. The sight of this beautiful locomotive weaving its way along the beachfront to arrive at its destination fills one with nostalgic memories of a bygone era. The engine, named 'Sir Malcolm Barclay-Harvey' after a Governor of South Australia, is one of twelve 520 class engines built at the Islington workshops in South Australia, weighing over 200 tons and delivering 2,600 horse power.

We feel we are indeed very fortunate to live in such a wonderful spot with a very temperate climate, where we can sit and watch the changing moods of the sea as the waves roll in to the South Coast, or go for a pleasant walk around Granite Island and observe the fairy penguins as they return to their rookeries at dusk. There are also several conservation parks nearby where we can enjoy vegetation in its natural state.

From: Betty Dempsey, Victor Harbor, South Australia

I live in Hobart and I love it.

I'm ten minutes' drive from the Post Office of a capital city, with all of a capital's advantages and none of the hassles. No pollution, parking problems or pushing people. My house sits in a grove of fifty-foot-high trees, bright with bird songs and bursting with buzzing blossoms. In season I can pick fresh apples, peaches, apricots, lemons and strawberries from my own and my friendly neighbours' gardens.

Two minutes' walk and I'm on the banks of the mighty Derwent River, a mecca for yachts, its huge deep water port allowing ships as big as the QE2 to poke their noses into the end of the main street. Half an hour's drive from my front door and I can be on the snowclad summit of Mount Wellington, or strolling along untouched ocean beaches with huge shark-free unpolluted rollers pounding onto miles of pure white sand.

Only two hours' drive gives me the choice of massive mountain ranges, lakes and rivers leaping with trout, or the primeval forests and wild rivers of our world heritage wilderness area. For entertainment we have Australia's oldest and most beautiful live theatre, the Theatre Royal, one of the finest Symphony Orchestras, and for the young in heart live bands, discos, nightclubs and a casino.

For discerning palates we have dozens of excellent restaurants serving the national foods of practically every country in the world and our local seafood is unrivalled—oysters, scallops, crayfish, sea run trout and Atlantic salmon flipped direct from water to pan. What's more, no restaurant is more than twenty minutes away and you'll find free parking at the front door.

But you're so isolated I hear you say. Phooey! I can fly to Sydney quicker than you can drive from the outer suburbs to the centre of Sydney.

But it's so cold you say. Rubbish! Hobart is cold only by reputation. We have a temperate climate with extremes neither of hot nor cold. With much higher than average hours of winter sunshine, my home is warm without any artificial heating and when the sun goes down there's the joy of a glorious open fire.

Who could ask for more?

From: **Gwyneth Dixon, Sandy Bay, Tasmania**

I live at Santa Teresa Mission (Little Flower of the Desert), around one hundred kilometres south-east of the Alice—just on the edge of the Simpson Desert. It is approximately 237 square miles in area—serviced by the Flying Doctor, School of the Air and RATS (Remote Area Television Service)—ABC of course!

Our population floats around 400-440 people and these are the Arunde folk. Our community boasts a swimming pool, a retail store, power station, school, hospital, church and community club with trampolines, indoor basketball court, juke box and video games. All the community are accommodated in houses that have been built by the people and they also run all of our facilities.

I used to run a garage/repair shop here for four years with the help of two Aboriginal mechanics. But now I run a courier service from the community to Alice Springs—three days a week—and carry mail, banking and communications to the different government departments.

We have just started a community development employment program where those people who do not have jobs and receive unemployment benefits work for their money. It appears to be working well and has instilled an amount of pride back into the people who suffer quite easily from 'shame' if they're not working and paying their way.

So this is where I live—not because I have to but I cannot find another place that gives me the satisfaction that I receive from the surroundings and the people.

From: **John Stevens, Santa Teresa Mission, Northern Territory**

Woodford Island is on the Clarence River, about halfway between Grafton and Yamba. It is about twenty-six miles long and nine miles across. It is said to be the largest inland river that has a mountain range in the Southern Hemisphere.

My family and I rent a little farmhouse and are in the process of cleaning up our two and a half acres of bushland that we are buying off our neighbours. We plan to build our mudbrick home 'among the gum trees' over the next few years.

We are sharefarming with our neighbours a small acreage of fruit—grapes, passionfruit, berries, more as a lifestyle than a business venture. We have lovingly grown many varieties of fruit trees and natives to be planted out this spring.

I love our home in this corner of God's own land. The flat dairy country is mostly turned over to cane and cattle now, but our little back paddock here has a large swamp area which is home to a pair of black swans that return every year to nest. Brolgas and jabiru visit often and perform their mating dance. Bird life abounds and it is not unusual to identify twenty to thirty different birds a day.

Our small school of twenty-two children and two dedicated teachers (one Canadian, on an exchange program at present) is situated on the 'Mighty Clarence' and our kids enjoy lots of outings that most big schools would miss out on. Recently we hired two luxury river cruisers and spent a day cruising around the island. At the moment the school children are constructing a picnic area on the river bank under the jacaranda trees for passing tourists who may enjoy to drop a line whilst taking in the picturesque views.

From: Vivienne Harris, Woodford Island, New South Wales

In December 1988 my daughter and I bought a house on the outskirts of Bungwahl in New South Wales. Although very fond of the open air we had always lived in towns and cities. The house stands in a two acre paddock and we have a salt water creek which runs into Smiths Lake and also a fresh water dam. Our nearest neighbour is half a kilometre away.

The creek is teeming with small mullet which we feed with bread and the dam also has a large number of fish about an inch long. We think that there are also mullet which breed and swim into the creek in heavy rain. In twenty weeks we identified thirty-seven different birds, including the azure kingfisher, scarlet honeyeater, Eastern rosella, king parrot and satin bower bird. We also have kookaburras, peewees, spur-winged plovers, fairy wrens and butcher birds.

In our first week we had a visit from two wood ducks, also called the maned goose, and by feeding them with seed and corn they have brought their relatives to a total of twenty-four. They have become very tame and in due season we expect an influx of ducklings.

The soil is heavy clay and in the rain the land is very wet, but we have drained some of it and established a native plant garden and a kitchen garden by laying poles on the turf in rectangles. We do no digging, and placed paper and cardboard on the turf and covered it with mowings from the paddock. We covered this with lawn mowings, kelp, lake weed, leaves, rotting rushes and anything else that we can collect including horse and cow manure. We have three compost bins which

WHY I LIVE WHERE I LIVE

WHY I LIVE WHERE I LIVE

WHY I LIVE WHERE I LIVE

WHY I LIVE WHERE I LIVE

WHY I LIVE WHERE I LIVE

WHY I LIVE WHERE I LIVE

WHY I LIVE WHERE I LIVE

WHY I LIVE WHERE I LIVE

e a tonne about every six weeks and these are made up with layers of the
 ping material and kitchen refuse. This is placed on top of the layers and we
 directly into the half decomposed material. This is contrary to all the
 nendations in the gardening books but it seems to work. It does away with
 deal of the hard labour and, at eighty-six years of age, this is a real bonus.
In twenty weeks we grew eighty lettuce, ten kilos of potatoes, ten kilos of climbing
beans, radishes, spring onion, and silver beet, and growing now we have all of
these plus sprouting broccoli, broad beans and leeks!

From: **Ernest Bristowe, Wamwarra Creek, New South Wales**

I don't live in Australia, I don't even live close. My home is a small island just
two kilometres wide and almost five long, rising 300 metres above the South
China sea. I live just thirty kilometres south of Hong Kong. The island is just
outside of the Regional Boundary of Hong Kong. So, in fact, I really live in China,
on the island of Oi Ling Ding, which translates to (Oi) Outside (Ling Ding)
Lonely Island. The island is one of a group of islands that dot the sea approach
to Hong Kong. The main industry is, like most of the surrounding islands, fishing,
and every day I can see the traditional Chinese junks heading out to sea from the
only village. The shape of the junks hasn't changed from the traditional shape,
only the sail and mast are missing and a large, marine motor roars below the deck.

I like the island. It is made up of granites. I'm the manager of the only quarry
on the island, supplying aggregate to the building industry in Hong Kong. I employ
over one hundred workers and they speak a great variety of languages, Mandarin,
Cantonese and a strange dialect called Hakka. I find the Chinese very friendly
and easy to get along with. From where I live on the island I have a magnificent
view overlooking the South China Sea, and some neighbouring islands. Near my
door is a mulberry tree with ripe black berries that stain the hands of those game
enough to pick them. I like this island, but it will never replace the big island
well to the south.

Every Sunday morning a little piece of Australia arrives in this corner of the
world, through the Perth hf radio. The locals may think I'm strange as I listen
through the hiss and crackle and the often fading reception, but I don't care; little
do they realise that the very kitchen they are standing in is transported, every
Sunday morning, to hundreds of kitchens just like it, the length and breadth of
our great wide land. I don't feel like I'm thousands of miles away. I'm just the
other side of the radio.

From: **Geoff Osborne, Kowloons, Hong Kong**

WHY I LIVE WHERE I LIVE